SEARCHING FOR MEANING

Searching for Meaning

A Religion of Inner Growth for Agnostics and Believers

BY

MARGARET ISHERWOOD

Macrae Smith Company

Philadelphia

TO DOROTHY
Mors Janua Vitae

The world of things we perceive is but a veil
Abraham J. Heschel

FOREWORD

"It seems as though a little more and we shall find out why we live, why we suffer.... If we only knew, if we only knew..." says Olga, in Chekhov's *The Three Sisters.*

Once we did know. We had a religion that gave us neat and definite "explanations," and it did not occur to us that these might be questioned. Scientific thinking, which encourages inquiry in all fields, is largely responsible for the breakdown of blind belief in what authority teaches.

The results of the breakdown have been both good and bad. It is good and desirable that man should learn to think for himself if life is to move forward. It is bad and dangerous if, as a consequence of too-shallow thinking, he sinks ... to the crude materialism of the elephant who cried "Each for himself and God for us all" as he danced among the chickens, feeling that as there was no God and no Hell to punish, nothing mattered. It is also bad if, being a more sensitive type, he resorts to suicide as the only way out of misery, despair, and an existential vacuum.

It is the theme of this book that the religion of the future must be set in a much larger and more comprehensive framework than that which has thus far been proffered by any church; that the search for truth must include both a deeper study of the inner world of man, his savagery and his sainthood, and a greater knowledge of the universe around us and its evolutionary significance. This is why I have said the book is for both believers and agnostics.

Mankind is slowly groping its way toward a world community. A world community needs a world religion that enables men to feel that they belong together, whatever their superficial differences; that satisfies the hunger for meaning and the hunger for the Unseen.

Such a religion will not be, as is sometimes feared, an amalgam of all others; it will be founded on faith in THAT which transcends all others: the Holy Spirit of Life.

At present man's imagination and spirit of adventure are directed toward distant planets in outer space. The last enemy to be destroyed is not space but death and suffering. This can be only when man has learned to direct his attention and his adventurous spirit inward, explored his own capacities for evil and for good, and discovered how to take the great evolutionary process a step forward toward a higher level of consciousness.

CONTENTS

FOREWORD

PART I: Meaning Through Growth
    I. *Personalia*   15
   II. *Roads to Meaning*   23
  III. *Inner Growth*   32
  IV. *Hindrances to Growth in Childhood*   35
   V. *Aspects of Adolescent Growth*   38
  VI. *Growth through Self-knowledge*   47
 VII. *Growth from the Deep Self*   54
VIII. *The Goal of Growth*   60

PART II: Meaning Through Religion
  IX. *Some Contemporary Interpretations of Religion*   67
   X. *The Great Hypothesis: God the Father*   79
  XI. *Jesus as Prototype*   94
 XII. *Another Dimension (God the Holy Ghost)*   106
XIII. *Religious Unity in Doctrinal Diversity*   117

PART III: Meaning Through Transition
 XIV. *Tradition and Transition: A Growing Fellowship for Growing Minds*   131
  XV. *The Great Transition: The Scientific Approach*   145
 XVI. *The Great Transition: The Inner Significance of Death*   153

EPILOGUE   161

APPENDIX I
  Religious Education   162

APPENDIX II
  Some Sources of the Enduring Tradition   166

INDEX   168

PART I

Meaning Through Growth

CHAPTER I

Personalia

Stages in the Journey from Doubt to Faith

Some good men have completed their universe. They believe all the
answers are in. Their thinking stopped with their graduation from college, where they may even have been told not to read anything that
might disturb their faith. Then comes a crisis, tragedy, and they do not
know how to meet it because the framework of their creed is too
small. "God" seems pitiless. He does not answer prayer; the neat little
structure theologians have built up about him collapses because it allowed no place for questing, gave no encouragement to independent
thinking. It was just an edifice built of doctrinal bricks rather than a
prism to catch the light from beyond.
OUSPENSKY

Every truth apprehended by finite intelligence must by its very nature
only be the husk for a deeper truth.
SPURGEON, *Mysticism*, p. 9. C.U.P.

There must be a large number of people who went through a
similar experience to that which befell me in my late teens,
though it may be doubted whether loss of faith is such a trau-
matic experience today as it was fifty years ago. Asking questions
is now more generally encouraged from childhood onward, and
many more interests compete with religion for our attention.
At the same time, thoughtful people of all ages find themselves
wondering about life.

There is a deep longing to know whether there is a God or at
least a "something" that gives significance to the whole process,
especially when faced with suffering: one's own, and the weight
of suffering everywhere. There is also a deep need to feel that it

matters, *sub specie aeternitatis,* how one lives, that it is really important to try to discipline the tiger and the ape within us and to contribute to life whatever lies in our power.

It is psychologically and spiritually dangerous to meet these needs or answer these questions in terms of a rigid and debatable theology. To do so is one of the most effective ways of emptying out new life with the "bathwater" of outworn dogmas. "Believe nothing because you have been told it." the advice of the Buddha to his disciples, was extreme but wiser than the opposite methods of early indoctrination advocated by Ignatius Loyola: "Give me a child till he is seven years old, and I will give him to you for the rest of his life."

Faith Lost and Found

In my late teens the system of beliefs forming the mold that contained my faith in life crumbled overnight. In actual fact the disaster could not have been as sudden as it appeared. Behind the scenes the acids of modernity had been at work for some little time but I had unconsciously erected a barrier against them. When the barrier broke the result was devastating, for the narrow biblical theology in which I had been nurtured was said to contain the fixed and unalterable truth for all time, and I did not know where else to turn for illumination or guidance. If this story of evolution was true, then the Bible was not. The ground gave way under my feet. I was in what is now called an "existential vacuum," a vacuum caused by the loss of any meaning for existence.

Cambridge did nothing to resolve my dilemma. My emotional foundations had been overthrown, and part of me continued trying to reestablish the Father-God who had been such a support and comfort during the long and dreary years at an unmirthful boarding school for the daughters of poor clergy. I was told by a fellow college student that I should never be a good philosopher if I did not abandon such wishful thinking: and from all my professors and their teaching I imbibed the impression that reason alone could be relied on as the way to truth. They may not have intended this, but I did not intend to be "duped" a second time, and reason seemed to give the only security against this. I did, however, sometimes consult with ministers. All were alike in making religion primarily a matter of belief, and as I could not coerce myself into believing something that was not proved, even though I felt guilty for not believing, I seemed to get nowhere.

Yet of course I was getting somewhere without realizing it. There was Pascal's strange paradox: "Thou wouldst not seek me if thou hadst not already found me," which must mean something and which suggested one was on the right track so long as one was seeking. But it was many years before I ceased worshipping the goddess reason as the *only* avenue to truth, and before I came to realize that there were other orders of knowledge as well as factual, and other modes of knowing than by the intellect. It took many years to abandon the futile attempt to find God at the end of a syllogism and to understand that feeling-experience could bring a kind of knowledge just as valid as knowledge of scientific or mathematical facts and no more to be doubted than these.

One of the most important of my "facts of experience" occurred very early in life, but its memory had been wiped out for some time, and later with loss of faith I became too involved with God the Father to pay much attention to a "mere" experience. In my old age that experience has fitted into place and become more important than anything I learned from books and University lectures.

It came about as follows: As a young child I was extremely fortunate in having free contact with the beauty of the earth, with woods and meadows, hills, lanes and a stream on whose banks grew forget-me-nots, willow-herb and lacy meadow-sweet. It was my delight to wander in these meadows. On one quiet Sunday afternoon at the age of nine I carried a baby sister down the sandy lane at the end of the garden.

Crossing the stream by the stepping stones, I laid her down under some sweet-smelling lime trees that were in bloom. Everything was very quiet save for the burbling water and the lazy munching of the melancholy cows. I was not thinking of anything in particular, but I must have absorbed the total ambience very deeply, for after nearly seventy years it is all still quite clear and still "holy ground."

The "Thing" happened suddenly but quietly, as if I had awakened from a dream. It is well known that we have no language in which to describe the experience of the noumenal.

> To those who know Thee not, no words can paint
> And those who know Thee know all words are faint.

So, like the prophet Ezekiel, I must fall back on symbolic terms and say, "The Heavens were opened," or, "It was as if a veil had been drawn and I saw the far country," which was not "far" but all around, filling me with wonder and gladness.

I remember saying, "Now I know what Heaven is like." Then I found myself repeating the twenty-third Psalm: "He maketh me to lie down in green pastures; he leadeth me beside the still waters." I had a vague feeling this must somehow be connected with what they were talking about in church — little as I ever understood of that save for a few Scripture passages of outstanding beauty.

When the moment had passed I seem to have thought no more about it. I had often had somewhat similar moments, as with the discoveries of the first snow-drop, the apple blossom in spring and the translucent yellow maple trees in autumn. The aesthetic and the mystic are very close, and the one can obviously prepare the way to the other without necessarily taking one "through" into the transcendent. Both, for those who want to express it that way, can be called experiences of "God."

But I did not know that. "God" for me was the name of a person who was my loving Father in Heaven. Later, when I was uprooted from that paradisiacal environment and shades of the prison house began to close, I needed this loving Father badly and derived great comfort from his existence and the assurance that he had everything under control and would eventually exchange this vale of tears for eternal bliss if one obeyed the command to "Endure hardness as a good soldier of Jesus Christ."

It was a grim philosophy but perhaps a less unwise extreme than indulgent permissiveness. In a way I believe that it served me well until I left school and made the shattering discovery that there were people who did not believe in any of it.

The discovery was altogether too sudden. A more intelligent religious education, even in adolescence, would have prepared me for new ways of looking at things and would have explained that one must, all through life, grow and outgrow earlier ways of thinking and feeling; that as we grow toward greater maturity, deeper and fuller meaning will continuously unfold. It was a sorry thing that I should have spent so many years hunting for childhood's personal God when all the time I had known that experience of *Le Milieu Divin* in the meadows. It was strange that I should "know" the truth that *this life is not all,* and not know that I knew it, still less be able to relate it to the theology of the churches.

This is why I suggest that today, instead of endlessly debating the existence of God the Father, the Supreme Being, we make clear that, since nobody can know whether such a "person" exists, we use the term "God," if and when we use it, as a symbol for the highest we know and that we should explicitly say that we are so using it; that we should, like the Buddha, leave aside all argument about God's existence and concentrate rather on those things with which God, if he exists, must be primarily and profoundly concerned, with self-transforming and the increase of wisdom and understanding, with significant living and dying, with truth and goodness, beauty and love. Such concentration would undoubtedly please him more than disputation concerning his existence, singing his praises, or begging his forgiveness.

A Hindu sage once said: "When a Westerner is faced with a theological problem he says, "I will consider this intellectually." The Hindu says, "I will try to raise my level of consciousness." The Hindu way is the more sensible, because when the level of consciousness is raised we can see further and see things differently. As Paul truly said, as we are at present we can only see "as through a glass darkly" and can only know "in part."

This is one of the most difficult steps in growing toward maturity, the relinquishing of our treasured "certainties" and accepting the fact that much of our knowledge can be only partial. Of Blake's poem "The Tiger" a child remarked, "It's nearly all questions." That is also true of life; there are more questions than answers, and when the answers do come through, they often arrive in unexpected ways from unexpected sources, so that we do not always recognize them.

Paul also said that when he became a man he put away childish things. Many of us fail to do this or to help children to do it, especially with regard to our thinking about God. We cling to the childhood's image even when we regard ourselves as "grown up." Intelligent children are, by the age of seven, quite capable of beginning to understand the meaning of abstract thinking. Christian children hear in church that God is a spirit and that the Holy Spirit is the third "Person" of the Trinity. This is meaningless, and unless they are helped to put some content into the word "spirit" and to seek out its presence operating both in the external world and in themselves, it may remain meaningless through life. The first step is to distinguish between concrete and abstract, between visible and invisible realities. That things like love and wave-lengths are real although they cannot be seen is an important discovery for a child trying to get a more intelligible concept of God than "the Man up there." It means that spirit too can be real, but, like love, can be known only in its operations and its effects.

When tragedy descends, the usual response of people with a personal and perhaps an anthropomorphic concept of God is to ask "Why? Why did this have to happen to me? Why did God allow it? He is omnipotent and so could have stopped it. 'Not a sparrow falls without his knowing,' So, Why?" Since there is no answer to such questions, the necessity of outgrowing the personal and understanding the spiritual concept of God is obvious. Otherwise the preacher is inevitably manufacturing atheists.

How do we find God as spirit? A man struck suddenly blind admitted the temptation to give in to self-pity, but added "I find there is another force in me on which I can draw and which enables me to say, 'I can manage; I am equal to this.'" Quite young children can, without being priggish about it, understand that story and relate it to themselves.

Such understanding will reveal that what is called "God the Holy Spirit" is the force in us that makes for courage, humility and love. It is what St Paul meant when he referred to 'the power that worketh in us." (*Ephesians III, 20.*)

When religion is thus built up through discussion and on an experimental basis, it will not break down. In my case it had been based on authoritarian statements that must not be questioned because they had been "once and for all delivered." At the end of that long searching I decided that the teaching of Jesus remained valid but that the teaching of the church *about* Jesus was debatable, that this should therefore be taken symbolically and the deeper esoteric meaning of such things as the Christmas and Easter festivals be made clear. Some things are truer than the literal truth, and the significance of the symbol as a carrier of meaning was one of the things that helped to awaken me to the realization that religion is an inward thing and that the true significance of the mythos lies in its inner and hidden meanings, not in the recorded outer events. For example, the statement that Christ rose from the dead, understood symbolically, is capable of various interpretations that are meaningful for us quite independently of whether we happen to believe it literally or not. That is not the important thing. Taken literally it seems to collide with modern knowledge, and so the literalist discards the doctrine without concerning himself with hidden meanings—without ever realizing that life and death are both parts of a complementary process.

Carl Jung writes: "The danger that a mythology understood too literally, and as taught by the church, will suddenly be repudiated lock stock and barrel is today greater than ever. Is it not time that the Christian mythology, instead of being wiped out, was understood symbolically for once?" Incidentally he adds that "there is no need of the Easter event as a guarantee of immortality, because long before the coming of Christianity mankind believed in a life after death." (*The Undiscovered Self.*)

Another brick for the new structure I was slowly building for faith in life was the study of evolution. Let those who wished insist that it was a purposeless and purely mechanical process brought about by natural selection and the survival of the fittest—with chance variations; the fact remained that from the dust this process had produced a Socrates, a Jesus and a Shakespeare. This was something to fill one with a great wonder. It indicated that "something" was at work.

Yet another kind of country that began to develop my interest in "other dimensions" was the realm of the paranormal. As described earlier I had already, as a child, had a simple mystic experience of a "beyond." Now that parapsychology has at last been freed from the taint of "unscientific," one can begin to see the connection between mystic or cosmic consciousness and paraconsciousness, and the support given by the one to the other.

Lastly, the loosening of my tenacious hold on reason as the only avenue to truth was further aided by acquaintance with Eastern religions, especially Buddhism, which is generally regarded by the West as atheistic and therefore "not a real religion at all." And certainly, if religion means primarily belief in God, is not an atheistic religion a contradiction in terms?

Again the answer came slowly over the years: start at a new place. Abandon the attempt to prove the existence of a mysterious and incomprehensible "person" existing somewhere in outer space and build up faith in life on what can be known in experience. I saw that the language and imagery in which truth is expressed must vary with the stage of development; that there are "grades of significance," and that as we let go of Childhood's God, we can become more aware of those things in life that may justly be called divine, which induce in us what Rudolf Otto called "a sense of the holy" and Schweitzer called "reverence for life." In short, that there is a larger reality which transcends the phenomenal world, which can become known to us only as our personalities become capable of apprehending it.

In one of his letters to Minanlabain, A.E. (Lord Russell) wrote, "I believe the only news of any interest does not come from the great cities or from the councils of state, but from some lonely watcher on the hills who has a momentary glimpse of infinitude and feels the universe rushing at him."

CHAPTER II

Roads to Meaning

What the totality amounts to and where it is leading is a comprehension we are reaching for but have not yet attained. . . . In fact the fulness of reality may always elude us, and what we sense now may be as much as the human organism is equipped to take. To see it face to face could be overwhelming, and may require an evolution far beyond our present half-baked stage.

N. J. BERRILL, *You and the Universe*, Dodd, Mead & Co.

When all goes well, few people concern themselves with questions about the meaning of life. If endowed with health and reasonable material conditions, they may, especially in life's heyday, say with Browning:

How good is man's life, the mere living, how fit to employ
All the heart and the soul and the senses for ever in joy.

That is how we feel things should be, but as one writer put it: "By the age of forty, most people learn to thank God if they are only tolerably unhappy," and the author of *Ecclesiastes* once wrote: "Therefore I hated life because the work that is wrought under the sun is grievous unto me; for all is vanity and vexation of spirit."

Nietzsche said, "Man can endure any 'how' if he has a 'why,'" and Jung, as is well known, described his middle-aged clients as "suffering from the senselessness and emptiness of their lives" and crying in their despair, "I could bear anything if only I felt there was some purpose and meaning in it all."

It is not only the middle-aged who suffer from a lack of meaning. Many of the young are also asking: "What is life all about? What does it mean? What is it for?" These will be among the more philosophically minded, or perhaps those who have suffered too much and can find nothing to make life worth living. Sixth graders in a recent study by Edwin Cox are described as "bewildered in their quest for a satisfying interpretation of life, and as being deeply concerned with the meaning, mystery and purpose of existence."

An observer from Mars might not unnaturally suppose that the young people on earth are at the present time primarily interested in smashing the sorry scheme of things and creating something nearer to their hearts' desire. But even if and when that has been achieved, the question of meaning remains, for death and suffering remain, and these are not solved on the material level. Home and children may be destroyed by an earthquake, struck by lightning, drowned by flood or ravaged by disease. My husband may die or may leave me for another woman. If there is no philosophy that takes into account the inevitability of death and suffering, then there is nothing left when the personal relationships that gave life meaning have been destroyed. A material Utopia is not enough; Humanism seems to give no opening on to the transcendental to which man longs to feel himself related; and official Christianity is intellectually unsatisfying.

This century has been a bad one for the breakdown of faith. In the sphere of religion, largely due to the impact of analytical science, many have lost their belief in an omnipotent and merciful Providence and many others are what Matthew Arnold called "light half believers," holding onto a vague faith in "a sort of a kind of something," as one undergraduate expressed it. The Victorians may not have had much religion in depth, but at least they had faith in progress. Until 1914 there seemed to be no reason why they should not continue to go forward indefinitely toward the fulfillment of man's assumed perfectability. Helvetius proclaimed: *"L'education peut tout!"* Optimism was the prevailing note and Wordsworth sang:

> Good was it in that dawn to be alive
> And to be young was very heaven.

Alas, that dawn never turned into day, and the flower of youth was mown down like the grass in the mud and filth of Flanders. "Very heaven" was reversed overnight into its opposite, and belief in the inevitability of progress received a mortal blow from which mankind is still staggering. But we failed to learn the lesson. History repeated itself twenty years later and is now preparing to do so again for the third time. And although we realize that technical invention can be directed to evil ends as well as good, material progress advances ever more rapidly and the faith of some could be expressed in the phrase "*Technocracy peut tout.*"

But behind that shallow optimism is the growing realization that technocracy can be more destructive of life and beauty than constructive. The comment of the disillusioned Einstein might well be hung in every research laboratory; "Had I known what they would do with my discoveries, I would sooner have been a locksmith." So if we are going to find meaning in life today, we shall have to take a very much larger perspective and develop much deeper insight.

Such a perspective has in fact already been opened up for us. It is now scientifically established that man is an evolutionary phenomenon, the product of an age-long process that has brought him from the stardust to conscious awareness. We know that this process has been continuous and without a break from flaming incandescent gases all the way to the spirit of man. With the last, the thinking, layer, "the earth gets a new skin; better still, it finds its soul," as Teilhard de Chardin expressed it in *The Phenomenon of Man.*

This picture of mind and spirit as the culmination of nature's evolutionary endeavor gives meaning to life and a foundation for faith in it which has never before been envisaged by man in this particular way. It obliges us to see ourselves as parts of a mighty cosmic process in which static "thinking" and inert ideas have no place. Since the life that pervades the whole must be at work in us also, it must require our conscious cooperation in its ultimate purpose—which, so far as we can see at present, is the evolution of ever higher levels of consciousness and personality. The work of Teilhard has been enormously helpful to many people in enabling them to recover faith in life by way of what used to be called a Natural Theology. Julian Huxley writes of him that he was "a man who uniquely succeeded in welding science and religion together in the white-hot glow of his own cosmic vision, the first great mystic who not only recognized the facts of evolution, but made of evolution the very substance of his vision. . . . He was a glorious optimist, and the generous vigor of his optimism sheds a devastating light on all the shallow pessimists of our age."

To some who do not share Teilhard's Christian orientation this may seem a surprising statement, but religion is wider than doctrinal Christianity, and the cosmic vision of the *milieu divin* offers a wonderful new basis for faith to those capable of it. For those who are not, science and religion are still "welded together" in the mysterious fact that somehow, and we cannot tell how, spiritual values and a sense of the holy have found their way into the process and point to a sphere beyond that of sense which Teilhard calls the noösphere, the sphere of mind and spirit.

The process has not gone forward in a straight line. Many of life's experiments have been failures, due often to the sort of mistake that man himself is now making—the mistake of over-specialization in one field at the expense of all-round development; overgrowth of the intellect at the expense of education of the emotional and spiritual.

The consequences of this imbalance are staring us in the face and may be disastrous. If, on the other hand, we can awaken to our predicament in time, man could grow as far beyond his present level of being as that is beyond the being of the amoeba. "We know not what we may be." In spite of all setbacks, the general trend of evolution hitherto has been in the direction of ever-greater complexity and sensitivity and higher forms of consciousness. A dog is more aware than a snail, a man than a mole. But higher consciousness gives more power of choice and an alarming responsibility for choosing well. To opt out of that responsibility, to "cease from mental fight" at this stage would mean devolution rather than advance.

Shortly before he died H. G. Wells gave this warning: "There is no way out for man but steeply up or steeply down. Adapt or perish, now as ever, is nature's inexorable imperative. . . . The odds seem to be all in favor of man's going down and out. If he goes up, then so great is the adaptation demanded of him that he must cease to be a man. Ordinary man is at the end of his tether."

That is the challenge. Changing the system will achieve nothing if human nature remains unchanged. Somehow we must become more than ordinary men. We have our direction and it is for us to decide whether or not we make the "Voyage to the Interior." The Life Force is available to us as a potentially indwelling Power by whose aid we may realize our full potential. If we take up the burden (along with the joy) of greater conscious awareness of ourselves, as well as of the external world; if we learn how to integrate and transcend unruly aggression, greed and fear, to value quality more highly than quantity, we shall be able to carry the Great Process forward, to find meaning in the experiences of life as we grow in understanding, and so fulfil our destiny on this particular minor planet. But to discover new planets or stars without discovering ourselves will avail us nothing.

The matter has been finely expressed by Julian Huxley: "Evolution shatters the pretence of human isolation and sets man squarely in his relation — and a very important relation — with the cosmos. It is the most powerfully integrative of concepts, forcibly and inevitably uniting nebulae and human emotions, life and its environment, religion and material nature, all into a single whole. The facts of human evolution, once clearly perceived, indicate the position we men should take up and the function we are called upon to perform in the universe. "Stand there" they say, "and do thus and thus." If we neglect to do as they order, we not only do so at our peril, but are guilty of a dereliction of cosmic duty."

That is a strange concept—"our cosmic duty." What can it mean? And can it ever be a sufficiently powerful motive for effort? Duty to family, school, country, church,—these are intelligible terms and reasonably manageable objectives. We are even beginning to awaken to the idea that we have a duty to the entire human family since we are "all members one of another"; even a duty to treat with care and respect our planet and all living creatures upon it. But the cosmos! Surely that is going rather far. Yet a worker in outer space has recently told us that we are all suffering from "cosmic provincialism," so it would seem that if we want to find meaning in the universe and not just on our own speck of it, we now have to stretch our minds still further and try to envisage the whole as one vast interrelated organism whose life flows through all, and to see ourselves as minuscule parts of the "Organism," able to make an effect just as an invisible cell can make an effect in the entire human body. We have been stopping short with our own planet.

Richard Buckminster Fuller has described a personal experience of the meaning of "cosmic duty," that is, of the sense of a moral imperative inherent in the nature of things. It came to him not so much from a contemplation of the evolutionary process as direct from life itself, an imperative which prevented him from committing suicide. He was at such a low ebb in his career, his financial position and his personal relations that there seemed no point in going on. Having made "a complete mess" of his life, he felt he was left with just two alternatives. He could either end it all and so give his wife a fresh chance with someone better than himself, or try to find a new way of life in which he could devote himself to something greater than himself. He made what he called "a blind date with principle." Standing one night on the shores of Lake Michigan, trying to face things out, he found himself saying: "You do not have the right to eliminate yourself; you do not belong to you; you belong to the universe."

Fuller did not attempt to trace the source of these words. They came to him as authoritative and that was enough. The Logotherapist—a healer who takes into account the spirit of man—would tell him that they came from a part of his deep self of which he was not yet conscious. The sense of not belonging to oneself confirms the intuition of the poet that "No man is an island, entire of himself." That being so, no man can say "My life is my own; I can do as I please with it" because, being a part of the whole, what he does will affect the whole. Therefore the realization of this intimate relationship should result in an awakened sense of responsibility toward the whole.

Many people have known, in a greater or lesser degree, an experience similar to Fuller's, an experience that the universe itself is somehow alive, that he is an organic part of it and can receive messages from it. Among the ancient Hebrews it was customary to refer to such messages as "the Voice of the Lord."

The modern rationalist, believing that reliable knowledge can be had only by the intellect, dismisses mystic experience as a form of "wishful thinking" and sometimes his skepticism may be justified. But the genuine mystic would also disagree with the rationalist, because he knows that to deny the validity of his experience would be the ultimate disloyalty.

What he knows, however, is of a different order of knowledge from that arrived at by logical reasoning. It is not to be described in words except to say that it brings the vision of a world that lies behind and beyond the world of sense, and the vision inspires a sense of awe and of great and holy wonder; it induces ecstasy in the experiencer and gives the utter assurance that all will be well.

Such experience has characterized many of the world's greatest thinkers and poets, including Euripides, Plotinus, Boethius, Eckhart, Bruno, Spinoza, Goethe, Whitehead, Shankara, Kabir, and Tagore. Indeed there is something of the mystic in every great scientist, poet, artist, musician and writer. It is "that" which enables him to see further and deeper than other men and to open the door to new insights for them. "Each time I put down the *Iliad*," writes Kenneth Rexroth, "I am convinced that somehow ... I have been face to face with the meaning of existence."

The experience may be but "a timeless moment," but it is a moment of truth. While it lasts, all doubts about the meaning of existence vanish. The "beyond" of which it speaks is not, of course, a geographical location. The mystic Jacob Boehme, when asked "Where does the soul go after death?" replied, "There is no need for it to go anywhere." It is a matter of seeing differently and seeing a "more." As with the butterfly after its final metamorphosis, it is in the same world, differently perceived. The ultimate reality or "noösphere" surrounds us, like the atmosphere, "closer than breathing, nearer than hands or feet," but we are not yet very sensitive to its presence or to the fact that in it "we live and move and have our being." We tend to make the false supposition that the world we know is all. This is because the "world invisible" is hidden from us by the limitations of our senses and our understanding. Aurobindo, the Indian mystic, says in *The Life Divine,* "The universe appears as only a symbol or an appearance of an unknowable reality. . . . And yet, when we speak of it as unknowable, we mean, really, that it escapes the grasp of our thought and speech."

All this will, for some people, savor too much of the super-natural, which they cannot except. But if that vexed term were understood as denoting *an extension of the natural* rather than as something wholly different in kind, the dualistic difficulty would be, to some extent at least, resolved. It is obvious enough that our rudimentary condition makes it impossible for us to have more than partial knowledge, that we can see only "as through a glass darkly," that we grope our way, often feeling like lost travelers in a forest.

But this is no ground for despair, if we accept the assurance of the earlier travelers that "behind the visible world of dense physical matter, there exists a finer, more subtle and invisible world of spirit, a world from which everything has originated." These are the words of Alfred Russel Wallace, codiscoverer with Darwin of evolution.

When we remember what science now tells us about the commonsense or "real" world, it should not be too difficult to entertain the hypothesis that a finer and more subtle world does lie behind the veil of sense and does at times reveal itself to the mystic. Dr. Johnson kicked the stone in order to confute the philosophic "Idealists" of his day who did not believe in matter. But now scientists have given support to the "Idealists" by breaking down solid matter into invisible atoms, protons, neutrons, and other tiny particles, all said to be whirling around at prodigious speed. Were it not for the status of the scientist in our age, we should doubtless dismiss such information as incredible nonsense.

What applies on the physical plane applies on the spiritual; there are more things awaiting discovery than we dream of. From this it follows that we should not expect to find THE meaning of life but a continuity of unfolding meanings, which will reveal themselves as we travel. Our God may be too small, as Nietzsche said, but our question "What is the meaning of Life?" is too large. We should attend rather to life's question to us: "Are you prepared to grow, to learn, to become, to journey on toward the Light, accepting the uncertainties that are the necessary accompaniment of your immaturity?"

That is the task, and that is the nature of the pilgrimage: to train ourselves to attend and respond to the "force-field" of spiritual impressions so that they become as real or more real than the physical. The growth process will take us, slowly and surely, both toward the noösphere and toward our own true selves, which include more than the intellect.

The following chapters will consider some aspects of what is involved in the growth process.

CHAPTER III

Inner Growth

Here we are as in an egg.
HERACLITUS

Unless a man grows in his spiritual character in proportion to his gigantic technological stature, the future will be in danger. The great problems of humanity cannot be solved by general laws but only through the regeneration of attitudes of individuals. Each one should try to overthrow the old order within oneself. Each one requires to be renewed.
s. RADHAKRISHNAN, *Religion in a Changing World*

When Goethe was asked, "What is the meaning, the secret of life?" he replied, "That which the plant does unconsciously, do consciously." That is to say: "Grow."

To complete the answer he should have added that only as we grow shall we find meaning. Growth is the key, the way by which we arrive at a fuller comprehension of meaning; it is not itself meaning.

A young man once went to G. B. Shaw for advice on what he should do with his life. He was told, "Find out what the Life Force wants you to do, and do it with all your might." Not a very specific answer, but Shaw meant the same as Goethe, "Grow, and as you grow things will become clearer to you." The "Life Force" does not give specific directions as to whether one should be a bus driver or a bishop, a poet or a plumber, but insofar as one is faithfully growing, the direction will become clearer and meaning will unfold.

In the preceding chapter we have seen that the world *as it now appears to us* gives us only one among an unnumbered series of "grades of significance" and that the barrier to our perception of a higher grade is subjective and due to our immaturity of sense or thought. This fact can be simply illustrated from the early stages of life.

To a year-old child, a book, whether Shakespeare or Beatrix Potter, is something to tear up, scribble on, or perhaps to chew. But in a few years' time he has learned that black marks on paper stand as signs for words that can be read to him as stories. Or again, he may be shown a picture on which he learns to recognize particular objects such as man, trees, chopper. Later on, his imagination working on experience will enable him to give a meaningful interpretation of the same picture: "The man is going to chop some wood for making a fire so that his wife can cook the dinner."

The capacity for perceiving meaning varies not only from age to age but from one individual to another, as any teacher knows. During England's Shakespeare Week when the poet's 500th anniversary was celebrated with a new issue of stamps, a woman waiting in the queue remarked to her neighbor, "Making a lot of fuss over him, aren't they? I never saw anything in him myself."

A woman inspecting Turner's pictures remarked, "But you know, Mr. Turner, I never see sunsets like yours."

She received the mild yet devastating reply, "No? Don't you wish you could?"

Such cases illustrate the diversities of gift in man, but they also illustrate latent capacity undeveloped for one reason or another. What matters, however, is not that one should be better able than another to appreciate a picture or play or piano concerto, but that each one should be growing, as long as he is living, toward his own particular potential capacity. That we should do this would seem to be an imperative inherent in life itself, and the consequences of ignoring this imperative can be very terrible, as the writings of Kafka, Rollo May, Aldous Huxley and many others have shown, and as the appalling cruelties of this century have revealed.

The causes of failure to grow may be physiological or psychological or both. The consequences may be neurosis, psychosis, or some other form of regression. Quite apart from these casualties, many people who are adult in years and intellect are still infantile in their emotions because they were either unable or unwilling to make the effort involved in growth, preferring a condition of dependence and protection. The type that the psychiatrist Anton Boisen calls "the drifter" is headed eventually for the "Wilderness of the Lost." His distaste for effort makes him finally incapable of effort, seeking easy modes of satisfaction in drink or drugs. In refusing the effort involved in growth, he reaches a stage when he can no longer choose even if he wanted, and "drifts ever further down to dissolution and destruction. As disintegration continues, malignant character tendencies increase and the 'Descent into Hell' becomes inevitable."

The dropouts in prison, asylum and clinic give all-too-tragic evidence of the descent. Rescue work is sometimes effective, but preventive work is what is needed, and that is primarily in the hands of parents, teachers and ministers whose true function lies in nurturing the emotional and spiritual, as well as the intellectual development of those for whom they are responsible. There are still teachers and parents who think that character can be formed by verbal instruction, without stirring the imagination or relating their teaching to life.

"Man's nature is to grow," says Ira Progoff. "When he is not able to grow, the dynamic life process within him doubles back upon itself and casts its energies into disorder. . . . The choice before man is thus inherently one of extremes: either growth with its fulness of rewards in life, or stalemate with growing restlessness, confusion, and eventual breakdown." (*Depth Psychology and Modern Man.*)

CHAPTER IV

Hindrances to Growth in Childhood

If a man is a being inherently in growth, why is he still living in a chronic state of enmity, fear and confusion bordering on despair? The comment that "most men today live in a state of quiet desperation" is no doubt an exaggeration, but it contains too much truth for complacency.

What is wrong? If our business is growth, why do we not get on with it? A seed planted in suitable ground and given adequate nourishment will grow without further trouble. "I want to see men growing like that tree," remarked an enthusiastic idealist as he contemplated a beautiful cedar adorning the lawn. Well, why not? The answer is simple, as Ben Jonson pointed out.

> It is not growing like a tree
> In bulk doth make man better be.

Man is a vastly more complex organism than a tree. He is, potentially at least, a person, and must therefore accomplish the inner growth that will enable him to achieve personality. This means facing the fact that his being is a battleground between conflicting forces. A journey like that of the seed lies before him but on another plane, involving both higher and lower levels of consciousness.

Because of his greater complexity, his upward growth can never be the straightforward matter that it is with the plant, but we are slowly learning more about some of the ways in which it can be healthily nurtured and some of the ways in which it can all too easily be damaged. Great wisdom and artistry are needed on the part of parent and teacher in further-ing the one and avoiding the other. If this were widely recognized, most of our problems would disappear, for human life would be treasured; quality would matter more than quantity. No one would lightly undertake the stupendous and godlike act of creating another human being if he was totally unequipped for such an awesome responsibility.

When people become emotionally ill, unable to cope with life, unable to face suffering, the cause often lies in some early blocking of their growth process. They may have been frightened or required to bear more than was endurable, so the life-flow is obstructed. The individual is then like a car trying to go uphill with the brakes on. He may manage to get along and function somehow, but he often seems dead-alive and, as D. H. Lawrence put it, "Goes round putting out the sun for other people." He appears devoid of interest, and interest is the growing point for mental development. Without interest the capacity for creative and courageous living dries up and the soul-sickness of apathy takes over, perhaps for good. Interest cannot develop where there is absence of emotional security. Many psychological studies have been made that demonstrate the fatal effect on a child's development of feeling unwanted and unloved in the early stages of life, and it is now a common-place that love is as essential to a child's emotional health as is food and shelter to his body.

Creative spirit seeks to express itself in the life of every individual. Lack of understanding blocks this expression and may lead to neurosis, delinquency or suicidal defeatism.

History and literature abound with examples of the disastrous consequences of frustrated development and its effects "unto the third and fourth generation." Sometimes such frustration is caused by what passes for love when "I love you" really means "I want you." Such is the smother love of the devouring mother whose own emotional immaturity causes her to cling tenaciously by a "silken cord" to her offspring, thus destroying their personalities by refusing them the right to grow freely and with wholesome self-direction. How many sons have had their lives ruined by their possessive mothers; how many daughters have been indoctrinated to believe that it is their

moral and religious duty to abandon all thought of an independent life in order to be a companion to some elderly relative? Such exploited daughters tend, in their turn, to become
dependants on the emotions of others, for it is hard to live alone
if one has not found anything within oneself to live by. Kind
friends may suggest such hobbies as basketry or rug-making,
but these do not allay heart-hunger.

Sometimes the hampered individual can manage to struggle
through life, working laboriously on one or two cylinders
instead of his potential six. Others cannot make it and take their
own way out of what becomes a too weary and soul-destroying
effort. The following story is not unique: In college Dave was
worried about his exams and consequently was staying up late
and drinking freely. A fellow student wrote of him, "He was
apparently more hollow or scared or confused or something
inside than any of us knew. One night he took all the sleeping
pills he could find, and was taken to a mental hospital. . . . The
next day he was successful in his suicide. He somehow slipped
out at night, found a knife and slashed his wrists.

"Try to imagine the drive he must have had to do away with
himself. I can't; it is too far away from my own love of life.
But he was in that same state when he was living just down
the hall from me. . . . Why doesn't someone tell us about the
depths of life, and not just its niceties, and how to get along,
and how to get ahead! . . . I feel utterly confused and scared.
Shades of Nietzsche again! I feel as if all religion, even hope,
has departed."

CHAPTER V

Aspects of Adolescent Growth

The Splendid Urge

> The youth who daily further from the East
> Must travel, still is Nature's priest.
> And by the vision splendid
> Is on his way attended.
> Until at length he sees it die away,
> And fade into the light of common day.
>
> WORDSWORTH, *Intimations of Immortality*

However many stages we may recognize in the process of growth toward maturity, the important thing to realize is that well-being at any one stage depends on the healthy development of the preceding stages, and that to try to force the pace of a child's growth in order to save oneself trouble is, in the long run, self-defeating. How wise was the precept of the Sufi teachers: "To each according to what he can take in his current stage of development." How often has a small sensitive boy been packed off at a too tender age to boarding school under the delusion that "it will make a man of him." What it does will depend on the temperament of the boy, on the wisdom of the school, and on the warmth and stability of his early home background.

Given suitable nurture of mind and emotions, there comes a time when a child of his own volition wants to be a man and is ready to pay the price of entering a new stage. This is vividly illustrated in the statement of a young man of French Guinea when he was about to undergo the initiation ceremony common to his tribe.

"It was not without misgivings that I approached this transition from childhood to manhood; the thought of it really caused me great distress, as it did those who were to share the ordeal. ... But however great the anxiety, however certain the pain, no one would have dreamed of running away from the ordeal — no more than one would have dreamed of running away from the ordeal of the lions — and I for my part never entertained such thoughts. I wanted to be born, to be born again. I knew perfectly well that I was going to be hurt, but I wanted to be a man and it seemed to me that nothing could be too painful if, by enduring it, I was to come to man's estate. My companions felt the same; like myself they were prepared to pay for it with their blood. Our elders before us had paid for it thus; those who were born after us would pay for it in their turn. Why should we be spared? Life itself would spring from the shedding of our blood."

Most tribes and people have recognized this "splendid urge" of youth to go forward into life and have provided various forms of ceremony for its expression and its canalization toward the ends and ideals of the particular community. "Today I am become a man," says a Jewish youth after the ritual of Bar mitzvah. But one does not become a man in any important sense of the word by undergoing a ceremony, though it is true that one cannot achieve maturity unless willing to endure inevitable pain.

A more sophisticated society would not wish deliberately to introduce pain into a ceremony, but many young people choose to test themselves in some way. When asked why he had so unnecessarily tackled the terrifying north face of the Eiger, one young man replied, "You learn something about yourself," and he added, "We didn't reach the top but we didn't fail."

It is a debatable matter whether there is anything to be gained by bringing the young to breaking point simply so that they may learn what they can stand, or achieve a little more than anyone else has yet done. Ideally, endurance should be related to a worthwhile purpose. If physical prowess becomes an end in itself it tends to degenerate into a mere cult of the body which, as British educator Kurt Hahn said, might be "the negation of humility." It might also degenerate into fatuous forms of competitive record-breaking to prove who can dance for the longest number of hours or eat the largest number of eggs or win the most goals on the football field. In his own Gordonstoun school, therefore, Dr. Hahn wisely related physical valor to the goal of service in such spheres as coast-guard operations, mountain rescue and fire service. These not only help other people but provide a creative way of sub-limating aggression and of canalizing energy toward worth-while ends.

Recently we have been seeing a good deal of youthful energy and idealism expressing itself in vigorous, even violent, protests against the evils of authoritarianism, war, famine and poverty. It is a fine thing that youth should feel the urge to mend this sorry scheme of things and should expend their energy in trying to do so. But energy without knowledge and understanding, rebellion without a constructive program, is liable to run into trouble. "Energy," said Blake, "is eternal delight." Yes, but like the raw energy of electricity, uncontrolled by reason and discipline, it can wreak havoc rather than create good. Or again, the adventurous and idealistic youth confidently going forth to fight the dragon may run into unforeseen complications, un-suspected cruelties or indifference to his ideals. Then the danger is that he himself may grow indifferent, may lose sight of his "vision splendid" and become cynical, looking for others to blame.

The older generation makes the obvious target of his disgust, but they too, it should be remembered, once went forth to fight and die for freedom. "Now God be thanked who hath matched us with this hour" expressed the mood of all young volunteers in 1914—until the blinkers were torn off and the hideous truth about modern war was laid bare.

History repeats itself, and all we seem to learn from history is that we do not learn. The ideals of courage and of service to one's country have almost universally been put before youth as among the very highest of virtues, the noblest goal for loyalty and self-dedication. A vow was once taken by every young male Athenian as follows:

> I will not dishonor my sacred shield. I will not abandon my fellow soldier in the ranks. I will do battle for our altars and our homes whether aided or unaided. I will leave our country not less but greater than she is now entrusted to me. I will reverently obey the citizens who shall act as judges. I will obey the laws

which have been ordained by the national will. I will reverence our ancestral temples. Of which things the gods are my witness.

Splendid, stirring words which, as they were uttered, must have given young men a sense of self-worth and of knowing what life was all about and what they had to live for. But such a goal was both too small and too egocentric in its nationalism. And when Athens rashly went to war with Sicily and suffered a crushing and humiliating defeat, the patriotic ideal would turn to dust and ashes. Youth would be left rudderless, feeling himself with "nothing left to strive for, love or keep alive for." For the Athenian oath, I would therefore substitute the words which G. Lowes Dickenson addressed to modern youth in World War I:

> There can be no peace, not even a genuine desire for peace, until men realize that the greatness of a people is to be measured by the quality of life of the individual citizens. . . . If men had the power of living, they would neither endure to kill nor desire to die. . . . It is because our peace is so bad that we fall into war. . . . It is our false ideals that make for war. And it is the feebleness of our intelligence and the pettiness of our passions that permit such ideals to master us. We seek collective power because we are incapable of individual greatness. We seek extension of territory because we cannot utilize the territory we have. We seek to be many because none of us is able to be properly one. Once more we are witnessing now whither that course leads us. Once more we are witnessing the vast and vile futility of war. . . . Once more we shall have a chance of learning the lesson. Shall we learn it? I cannot tell.
>
> But I hope. I hope because of the young. And to them I now turn. . . . If you return from this ordeal, remember what it has been. Do not listen to the shouts of victory; do not snuff the incense of applause; but keep your inner vision fixed on the facts you have faced. You have seen battleships and bayonets, and you know them for what they are, forms of evil thought. Think other thoughts, love other loves, youth of England and of the world. You have been through hell and purgatory. Climb now the rocky stair that leads to the sacred mount. . . . Take up the thought and give it shape in act. It is for that you have suffered. It is for that you have gained vision. And in your ears for your inspiration, rings the great sentence of the poet [Dante]:
> "Free, right and whole is thy will, and it would be error not to act at its bidding. Wherefore I crown and mitre thee Lord over thyself." *After the War*

It is absolutely essential to mental health to have something to live for, something or someone to care for more than oneself. Life would otherwise be meaningless indeed. But if the love object is too small, too limited and transitory, its loss may leave one utterly bereft.

Arthur Miller, in *All My Sons,* describes a character whose love object was his family. When faced with the appalling consequences of allowing defective airplanes to be sent to the front, he excused himself on the grounds that otherwise he would have been ruined. "I did it for the family; there's nothing bigger than the family."

Quietly, his wife replied, "There is something bigger."

This truth eventually dawns on him when hears that his own son is one of the twenty-seven casualties. As he goes out to shoot himself, he says, "A man can crack too; a little too much pressure and he cracks like a defective cylinder." Then follows the realization: "They were all my sons."

So if neither patriotism, nor family, nor any personal relationship is entirely adequate for living, what is? Does the Christian initiation ceremony of confirmation offer a larger vision of service? It certainly tries to present an ideal more permanent than family or country, to teach a way of life that will triumph over all personal weaknesses and all outer circumstances. Yet the complaint is often made, "They tend to drop away after confirmation." Why? One reason is that the church vows taken tend to emphasize renunciation. Although the old ceremonial words sound impressive, it must be doubted whether they mean very much to the candidate, who no longer subscribes anyway to the doctrine that carnal desires are sinful. Goals and ideals expressed in such sweeping and archaic terms as, "the vain pomp and glory of the world with all the covetous desires of the same, and the carnal desires of the flesh," are too vague to be of much help. More specific guidance is needed, especially in the sphere of the "desires of the flesh," commonly referred to nowadays as sex impulses.

In this connection Suzanne Lilar, in *Aspects of Love,* emphasizes the necessity of being more specific. She writes: "In our society, preparation for love is not merely left to chance but is deliberately doomed to ignominious failure. A vast majority of men of the West approach the sexual act as barbarians might. The civilizing value of love can get the better of this barbarism, the practice and custom of love can refine and uncoarsen; but this is preceded by clumsiness, awkwardness, mistakes (sometimes irreparable), disappointments, irritations and revulsions, all of which an education in love would have avoided."

An education in love is of course a much larger and deeper thing than an education in sex, which is but one aspect of love. Modern "pop" singing centers around the theme of fleeting erotic love, and one wonders how much knowledge and understanding lies behind it.

Mrs. Lilar records a terrible incident that demonstrates how adolescent love, experimenting in conditions of almost total ignorance and lack of self-restraint, can rapidly degenerate and bring into play forces so primitive and formidable that they turn man into something lower than a beast and "love" expresses itself in unbelievably horrible forms of aggressive cruelty. In our own day a boy of fifteen, described by his teachers as "tender, gentle and sensitive," committed an appalling murder of the girl he loved, illustrating the dangerous proximity of the opposing forces within us. Self-ignorance can make it possible for us to slip from tenderness to brutality without realizing what is happening. The mind of man is indeed both a "savage and beautiful country." One has only to remember the wild and terrible orgies of the Bacchae, which formed part of the worship of the god Dionysus. The savage in man is projected onto his gods, as when Jehovah is made to say, "I the Lord create evil" *(Isaiah, 45, vii)* and the Hindus represent Shiva as both Creator and Destroyer. Certainly both forces are operative in life.

Two things need to be said. The inquiry into the terrible story of the two child lovers mentioned by Suzanne Lilar "established that Jan's sexual ignorance was amazing; he had absolutely no knowledge of what to do in order to make love to Ada." So he blindly followed the way of the sadist.

The answer might seem to be simple enough: give the necessary information, as did the primitive tribes at their initiation rituals. But the factual information is not enough. Suzanne Lilar says: "The idea of an erotic initiation is, of course, old and venerable. But while, in the past, such preparation has always had a sacred character, . . . modern sexual education has not. It is profane, rudimentary and disparaging."

By "profane" is not meant "irreverent" or "blasphemous" but "not belonging to what is sacred:" "outside the temple"—in other words, knowledge given as bald fact rather than as initiation into a great mystery that "carries the flesh into the spirit and the spirit into the flesh."

But no more than country, family, or friend is sex an all-inclusive goal for living. Is there indeed such a thing as an all-inclusive goal? Tennyson gave the right answer so far as direction is concerned: "We needs must follow the highest when we see it." But he did not and could not tell us how to be sure of what is the highest. There is often no clear-cut pointer to that, and the choice has to be made for whatever seems on the whole to be the more right, the less wrong. The result is that we may at one and the same time be subjectively right but objectively wrong. The fact noted by St. Augustine that "loyalties cut up against one another" can be a heartrending experience—as, for example, for pacifists in wartime.

The boy who in his grief cried, "Why doesn't someone tell us about the depths of life and not just the niceties?' was asking for something that cannot be told in words.

The depths of life can be known only through inner growth based on personal experience. A philosophy of life that includes death and tragedy is not to be had from a textbook or a lecture alone, though these may help. It is built up slowly through the years by those who sincerely want such wisdom and, like Odin, are willing to pay the price—not, like Odin, by sacrificing a physical eye, but by another kind of discipline that stretches the mind and will, as some are willing to stretch their bodies.

Discipline is another emotive and equivocal word. A trained condition is as necessary to the athlete in living as to the athlete in sport. A person of uneducated emotional life is liable to go "all to pieces," to "crack under pressure" like defective cylinders.

"The science of sciences and the art of arts," said Hesychius of Jerusalem, "is the capacity to master harmful thoughts. The best method and remedy against them is to watch with God's help for the appearance of their suggestion and always to keep the thought pure, just as we protect the physical eye, watching sharply for anything that might injure it and not letting even a speck of dust come near it." *(Texts on Sobriety and Prayer,* from *The Writings of Philokalia.)*

The suggestion of Hesychius may sound altogether too grim and bordering on an undesirable asceticism. Yet in view of mankind's predicament it merits attention, if only as a possible way for devising one's own yoga. Everyone needs a way of thought and behavior that will help to keep his life in order and to give some degree of control over it, even if we can never go so far as to say with Henley:

> I am the master of my fate,
> I am the captain of my soul.

As well as finding techniques for keeping his life in order, a young person needs to build a religious philosophy that makes sense of life; an outlook that will enable him to survive the loss of country, family, friends or doctrinal religion. This means becoming able to see the life we now know as but a stage in a much larger life; it means seeing oneself as a miniscule but nonetheless important cell in the mighty living whole. Anyone who has been inspired by the wondrous story of man's long evolution from the mud will feel gratitude to those who have worked so hard to reveal this story and a sense of responsibility for doing his share in furthering the great process. There is no other way to feel self-respect and a sense of self-worth in this suffering world, no other way in which to find it endurable, than by making sure we are doing all we can to carry things forward both in the outer world and within ourselves.

Struggles to conquer high mountains, deep seas and outer space will have to be matched by the struggle to conquer the unadmitted, and largely unrecognized, greed, malice and power-lust in ourselves. The splendid urge in the young to be of service and to remold the world in justice is too precious a thing to be wasted. But youth's education should include: (1) a study of human nature, beginning with one's own; (2) a study of the history of mankind that gives a sense of what has been involved in the long, slow growth from protozoa to man — the terrible barbarities and the glorious achievements; (3) a religious philosophy that will be able to withstand intellectual criticism and will infuse a sense of responsibility for carrying the life process forward—a realization that it is "better to light one candle than to curse the darkness," to create one constructive program than to try violent short cuts.

It is regrettable that an ever-increasing number of today's young Christians find no such psychology or philosophy in their churches. After hearing that they must grow out of the conception of God as "up" or "out" there, they kick with frustration when they are later told by somebody else to believe that God "sent" his Son Jesus Christ to earth to save sinners.

CHAPTER VI

Growth through Self-knowledge

Fruitless is the wisdom of him who has no knowledge of self.
EMERSON

In other living creatures, ignorance of self is nature; in man it is vice.
BOETHIUS, fifth century A.D.

Bishop Robinson has urged us to be "honest to God." We can do this only by being honest with ourselves, and this necessitates getting clear knowledge of ourselves. We have referred to the sort of disasters that can result from self-ignorance. We must now ask why knowledge of ourselves is so essential and so hard to acquire.

When one is confronted with the baffling question "Who am I?" there is often a sense of bewilderment. So far as external details are concerned, these can be found in a passport. But the inner "me"—what sort of being is that?

A common answer in the West sidesteps the question roughly as follows: "It is morbid to think about yourself. You should think about other people and what you can do for them. Then you will forget yourself."

Looked at superficially, this extravert attitude contains an element of truth. Some people are indeed much too concerned with their own feelings and affairs. Such a condition, however, is not caused by detached introspection but by the lack of it. The introspection that seeks for knowledge of what goes on in the human psyche in order to get a better understanding and control of oneself is not morbid. It is as scientific as the observation of an invisible polio germ, and just as important.

It must be very important indeed or such great teachers as Gautama, Socrates, Jesus, Montaigne, Jung, Freud, Adler and the rest would not have laid so much emphasis upon it. It was through knowledge of themselves that they were able to acquire insight and to give guidance to others. It was, for example, because Jesus had discovered in *himself* the temptation to take a short cut to power, possessions and prestige (the "devil" that tempted him in the wilderness was no *external* monster), that he was able to penetrate behind the mask of piety worn by the Pharisees, to perceive in them the Jungian "shadow" of greed and self-love dressed up as pious concern for the law of God.

But since Jesus is assumed by many people to be at least half god, let us take our next example from another fine individual whose normal membership in the human species has never been called in question.

No one would deny that Florence Nightingale was a splendid character who gave herself wholly and heroically to the service of others. Yet a failure of insight allowed her sister's emotional tyranny very nearly to ruin her remarkable career. The fact that giving in to the selfish demands of others is harmful to them, as well as to the one who is being exploited, is one of the most difficult things to learn. In 1840, Florence wrote in her diary: "A very justly successful physician once told a sister (meaning herself) who was being Devoured, that she must leave home in order that the Devourer might recover health and balance which had been lost in the process of devouring."

The "Devourer" in this picture was the elder sister Parthenope, who had kept Florence in a kind of emotional bondage for many years, making use of "illness" as a cover for her passionately possessive "love." The enslaved Florence described the doctor's talk with her as "a terrible lesson which tore open my eyes as nothing else could have done. My life has been decided thereby."

Official psychoanalysis was unknown in those days, but there have always been men of deep perception like Sir James Clarke, the doctor in question. Numerous are the examples of the harm that is done through self-ignorance. The great evil of war is not caused by any one person or one event but by a combination of causal circumstances, yet the final precipitating cause may be due to a more than usual lack of self-knowledge in one man; by his unawareness of the ambition, power-lust, resentment or envy by which he is driven. It is utterly essential that we get to know ourselves better in the future; that we cease to ignore that profound and pitying supplication from the Cross, "They know not what they do."

Why is it so hard to know? Why is there this barrier between conscious action and unconscious motivation? What causes this strange split in the human psyche so that we ask in bewilderment: "I wonder what made me say that? I didn't mean to. I'm sorry now." Or, on the other hand, "Why was I too cowardly to speak?" Beyond doubt there is a deep division in the psyche that makes it possible for one "self" to do or say what another "self" disapproves of.

How this division came about is a matter for speculation. In *The Ghost in the Machine* Arthur Koestler proposes the hypothesis that owing to some biological defect there is inadequate coordination between the thalamus or old brain, the seat of the instinctive emotions, and the neo-cortex, the seat of intelligence, the lines of communication being insufficiently developed. He writes: "When one contemplates the streak of insanity running through human history, it appears highly probable that *homo sapiens* is a biological freak . . . the result of some remarkable mistake in the evolutionary process. . . . Somewhere along the line of his ascent, something has gone wrong."

It is an interesting theory but hard to prove. Moreover, even were the biological lines of communication between the two brain centers to be remedied by the discovery of a biochemical pill, as is suggested, does it follow that psychological dissociation would cease, that we should no longer repress into the unconscious those things that we do not wish to remember?

Dr. James Hemming, author of *The New Statesman,* believes there is a more obvious explanation of the divided mind. He says: "It is not the brain structure that is at fault . . . it is the inadequacy of the nourishment in experience during the growth period — a faulty education at home and school." Here we are on surer ground. The distinguished research work of people like Anna Freud, John Bowlby and others into the emotional lives of infants has demonstrated clearly enough the harm often caused by insecurity and lack of tender loving care in the early years of life. Love is as essential to emotional health as is food to the body.

To begin with, the infant psyche (what there is of it) is an undivided whole. Gradually, in the course of the first two or three years, there dawns the consciousness of self, the ability to say "I," to recognize oneself as a focus of reference. It is when the wants of the child begin to clash with those of the adult that there is trouble. But so long as discipline is reduced to the necessary minimum and given always with loving skill, no harm is done. Only when the adult's standards are too rigid and too harshly imposed does the child start leading a double life, perhaps taking to lies and deceit in order to avoid disapproval and the loss of love.

In my own childhood it was possible to purchase a "false face" made of painted cardboard for a penny and to pretend that one's identity was concealed behind it. Nearly everyone must know the experience of having pretended on occasion to be something other than he really is. So long as he is aware of what he is doing, there is no split in the personality. But if the wearing of a persona or mask becomes habitual—as in the case of Dickens' Uriah Heep or in some of the Pharisees—then the individual tends to identify with it and to lose sight of his real self, which should be growing up in him through coming to grips with life's problems instead of escaping from them behind a false face.

Mr. X was a handsome and wealthy businessman in his late fifties, a churchgoer, a director of several companies and the father of an affectionate family. One day, to the shocked surprise of all concerned, he announced that he was going away to find himself. His statement "I have never been allowed to be myself" related back to childhood and an authoritarian father according to whose precepts and example he had lived his externally successful life. With death beginning to loom in the near future, he suddenly felt hollow. Everything he had worked so hard to build up around him seemed without significance. He felt lost because he had never found his true center or self.

The story is not uncommon, and literature abounds with similar examples—including Norah, in Ibsen's play *The Doll's*

House. The sorry state can be avoided only by learning to watch ourselves as we travel.

It may be asked, "But how can the self watch itself; how can it be at once observer and observed?"

The answer is that the self, no matter how lovingly nourished and wisely treated, soon ceases to be a single, simple entity. Paradisal innocence has to be left for the rough and tumble of life and no one can smooth absolutely all problems and sufferings out of the path for us. If these are met with courage and not run away from, a new function of selfhood, an "observer," emerges out of the complex of the total psyche, just as in infancy the conscious ego emerged out of unconsciousness. This new observing "self" now watches and tries to direct the ego self. It helps the individual to form a center around which all the confused, disconnected and conflicting aspects of the psyche should become organized. This center has been called the inner light, the immanent divinity, the true self, the beyond that is within. It may be but a small precarious flame, or, as in the saints, a steady lamp that never fails.

Knowledge of this part of the psyche is, to say the least, as important as knowledge of the savage tendencies in us which Freud has disclosed. Of what use is it to discover all the meanness, resentment and cruelty unless we also discover the power of the spirit in us to transmute this lower nature? Or "what doth it profit a man if he gain the whole world at the cost of his true self?" *(Mark VIII, 36.)*

"The life of man can be envisaged as a journey in which we pass from one stage to another. After the relative calm and simplicity of childhood come the bewilderments and problems of adolescence. If we work our way doggedly through these, we shall, in time, begin to find our priorities and discover within ourselves a center that will eventually integrate all the entangled strands of the total psyche and relate them to itself. This spirit-center is the goal of life. It not only unifies our dispersed condition: It connects us with "the center of all centers" that is Teilhard de Chardin's concept of God.

The transition from one stage to another in the journey of life is for most people very gradual, and there is no absolute break between one stage and the next. Even in infancy the mind is not a blank sheet, and the attempt to make pattern and meaning out of life starts in some children well before adolescence. Increasing maturity brings increasing clarity, and an erstwhile self-tormented and divided individual, such as Paul of Tarsus, becomes able to say, "This one thing I do," or, as the New English Bible has it, "My friends, I do not reckon myself to have got hold of it yet. All I can say is this: Forgetting what is behind me, and reaching out for that which lies ahead, I press toward the goal. . . ." *(Philippians III, 13.)* What was his goal? It was "to take hold of THAT for which Christ once took hold of me"—the Holy Spirit of truth and good. Paul admitted to having (like the rest of us) a divided personality. "The things I would not, them I do." And he confessed to having made bad mistakes in the past. But after he saw the light, he never lost his direction. He could have said with Ruskin: "I have often slipped, but have never turned my face." So we too—as self-knowledge enables us to see more clearly, to follow more nearly—we shall eventually "return to the place from which we started and know it for the first time." (T. S. Eliot.) It is the same place in wonder and beauty as seen through the eyes of the little child, but not the same in Edenic simplicity and innocence. For the new wholeness is created by the integration of life's complexities. It is wrought out of a lifetime's struggle and growth toward maturity: a maturity that will give us some illumination into the meaning of it all.

But there is no private salvation, for as well as being individuals we are parts of a great organic unity, "members one of another." Alexander Pope expressed the same truth in "An Essay on Man":

> All are but parts of one stupendous whole
> Whose body Nature is, and God the soul.

The immense difficulty of the task of self-knowing and self-transforming might cause us to shrink from it in despair but for the encouraging fact that hominids did eventually turn into men. What men may become we cannot say. All we know for certain is that, having achieved consciousness, further evolution depends on ourselves—on our ability to bring our proud intellects and unruly wills into harmony with the moral and spiritual aspects of our natures.

GROWTH OF THE SELF

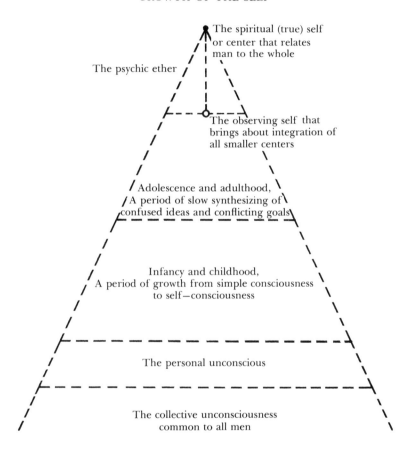

The spiritual (true) self or center that relates man to the whole

The psychic ether

The observing self that brings about integration of all smaller centers

Adolescence and adulthood, A period of slow synthesizing of confused ideas and conflicting goals

Infancy and childhood, A period of growth from simple consciousness to self—consciousness

The personal unconscious

The collective unconsciousness common to all men

The broken lines indicate that there is no absolute division between one stage of growth and the next, or between the spirit of man and the spirit of the universe

CHAPTER VII

Growth from the Deep Self

Modern civilization, with its emphasis on rationality and conformity, has separated man from the dimension of depth in himself and has weakened his intuitive capacities. It is contact with these resources that needs now to be developed. . . .

The reactivation of the natural process of growth is accomplished primarily by learning to participate more fully and harmoniously in the continual flow of imagery.

IRA PROGOFF, *The Psychology of Personal Growth*

We must be continuously on the watch for ways in which we may enlarge our consciousness.

ALDOUS HUXLEY

Hitherto growth has been spoken of as if it were a matter of conscious development; but, as we all know, we are something more than conscious beings. We know that—to speak in spatial terms—there are vast areas of the mind with which we have little or not contact save in dreams. Shakespeare's Prospero goes so far as to say "We are such stuff as dreams are made of," but it is very hard for the surface tip of the iceberg to know what the submerged nonconscious part of the mind is up to.

Freud's concept of an unconscious mind that is the abode of instinctive urges and repressed experiences is true so far as it goes, but it is not the whole truth. In the nonconscious mind, creativity is also at work and often seems to be trying to tell us something of importance through the medium of dream imagery. Many dreams appear to be nothing but meaningless and irrelevant nonsense, but throughout the ages men have felt that sometimes a dream is bringing a message to the conscious self. Where that is so, then "a dream not understood is like a letter unopened."

That there is a part of myself, my total psyche — if that is what it is — operating on its own and sending me images that "I" certainly did not originate, is a rather startling and exciting discovery. When an image is experienced as a carrier of meaning we call it a symbol. This means it has something to say if we can "hear" and understand. It is a great mystery, and it is not surprising that the people of Old Testament times interpreted the experience by saying, "The voice of the Lord came unto me saying . . ." Unfortunately there is a danger of mistaking one's own unconscious desires for the "voice of the Lord." But if today we prefer to say that, in addition to unconscious instinctive drives, there appears to be a creative and directive "principle" urging us toward wholeness, that does not lessen the mystery. The following example will illustrate the nature of the process.

I once had a brief dream in which I was standing at my window watching a queer sort of inverted and unbalanced balloon floating past. The strange thing about it was not only the inversion and imbalance but the fact that the square carriage or "body" was larger than the inflated ball of the balloon containing the gas which should enable the whole to rise (Diagram 1).

I awoke feeling puzzled and the thought came, "That is like me. My tired, heavy body gets on top of my spirit. How good if it were the other way round as it should be."

I thought no more about the matter, but a few days later when idly doodling with pencil and paper, I noticed that I had, quite unconsciously, enlarged the round bag of air and fitted it neatly inside the square "carriage" (Diagram 2), and the pleasing thought came, "Ah, that's better; you have squared the circle." I thought that this might be an illustration of Jung's "reconciling image" and that perhaps there was here a hint of a solution to the problem of the body-mind relationship.

Later in the day I found myself discontented with this image, which suddenly seemed flat and two-dimensional. It thereupon became nothing but the base of a beautiful tall spire which at first seemed, to hold the answer I was seeking. Life had other dimensions — the dimension of spirit which the spire represented

(Diagram 3). *Spirare* means to breathe, and breath symbolizes life. We aspire to that which lies above and beyond our humdrum lives and we are inspired by it.

These were good and satisfying thoughts. Supposing that the matter was now closed, I was surprised to find the same feeling of dissatisfaction returning a few hours later when the thought asserted itself, "This spire does not breathe; it is dead, like a pyramid."

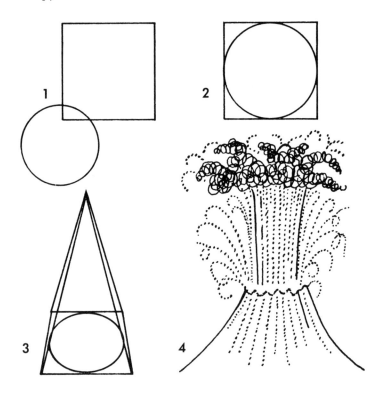

Thereupon it changed into a cone-shaped mountain, from which flames of fire leapt forth (Diagram 4). My first reaction was, "a volcano," and then, "Fire is alive as the stone spire was not, and fire is a symbol of the spirit." The Holy Spirit descended on the disciples at Pentecost in the form of "tongues of fire." John the Baptist said, "I indeed baptize you with water, but one mightier than I ... shall baptize you with the Holy Ghost and with fire," and "He maketh ... his ministers a flame of fire." This was evidently "the divine flame" that awaits our kindling. H. G. Wells wrote, "There is an undying fire in the heart of man; by that fire I live." But alas, the flame is precarious and can all too easily go out, quenched by the weariness of the body or the cares and miseries of the world, unless continuously tended and fed.

These were some of the thoughts that passed through my mind. After a time, the same feeling of dissatisfaction reappeared, for I saw that as well as being a symbol of the spirit of good and growth, fire could also be a terrifying and destructive force. Inflamed, passionate uncontrolled emotion seemed to me the most dangerous thing in man, making him capable of deadly evil and cruelty. Hell is biblically described as a lake burning with fire and brimstone. Fire, it seemed, is not a wholly or finally satisfactory symbol after all. Its energy, though a Promethean gift, is too raw and indiscriminate for "civilized" man.

With these thoughts it seemed to me that the cone-shaped volcano changed into a mound from which grew, in place of raging flames of fire, a tall and stately tree. I felt a deep content as I dwelt on this image and let it speak to me. The "tree of life" is such a universal symbol that I felt it must have much to say. I perceived the obvious significance in its dual relationship to sun and soil, receiving nourishment from both, its leaves reaching up and converting the sun's rays into one kind of food and its roots absorbing moisture and minerals from the earth. Man's life also had this dual aspect in that while needing earthly bread, he cannot live by that alone but needs the "bread of heaven" for spiritual health. In the second place, although the tree has trunk, branches, roots and leaves, these are all related, because the tree, unlike the fire, is an organism, and the vital sap circulates through every part of it.

I recalled a line in a poem by George C. Cook: "The leaves have life although unlike my own." How unlike? Obviously without my complexity and my consciousness. The tree is a lovely image of unconscious beauty and symmetry, and we can learn from it up to a point, but man has to go further—beyond both the mineral and the vegetative spheres and into the noösphere.

We have no difficulty in describing a tree, but man is a great puzzle to himself. "Who am I?" is an age-old question, and my mental screen was blank on the subject. But the words of the physicist Jeans came to mind: "The whole universe is waves, nothing but waves." Man is part of the universe; therefore he too must essentially be composed of electric waves. As he builds his personality during this earthly life, will his true spiritual self continue to function after death in some sort of "body" composed of invisible waves?

That seemed a reasonable hypothesis, but whatever in my unconscious had been sending the sequence of images now failed to produce any more. And this is not surprising, for, as Goethe said, "Man's faculties are not sufficient to measure the action of the universe." Yet it would be strange if the great evolutionary process were to end with man as he is when his body dies. No wonder that one thinker asked for the word "unfinished" to be inscribed on his epitaph, for at the end of this life we are only just beginning to understand who we are and to realize that our business in this stage of being is to prepare ourselves for entry into the next.

Some years later, after experiencing more of the struggles and sorrows of life, I began to feel that the perfectly symmetrical tree of the diagram was not an accurate symbol of life as it really is. I called to memory the striking Monterey pines in California, battered and twisted by the sea winds, yet still holding their own and beautiful even in their deformed condition. These seemed to give a more correct statement of the battle of life, for "Frail are those trees that have known only a sunny valley." Robert Frost expressed the connection in "Tree of my Window":

> But tree, I have seen you taken and tossed,
> And if you have seen me when I slept,
> You have seen me when I was taken and swept
> And all but lost.
>
> That day she put our heads together,
> Fate had her imagination about her,
> Your head so much concerned with outer,
> Mine with inner, weather.

What is to be deduced from my unexpected and unwilled sequence of images? First, that the bit of myself I normally know and refer to as "I" is not the whole. My conscious ego-self could no more elicit and direct this imagery than it can digest my food or heal a broken leg. The images come into my mind and "I" become aware of them — just as an idea may "occur" to me "out of the blue."

We say, "I suddenly had a bright idea." But I do not invent my ideas. I perhaps prepare my mind to receive them by working my way around a problem, and then it may happen that things "fall into place" and I "see" — I understand what it is that has been given by the "not-self"; that is, presumably, by some part of my total psyche I know nothing of but can cooperate with by making ready the ground for its message and being in a state of alert passivity, or relaxed attentiveness, in which I can become aware of it.

We use such terms as "integrative thought," "insight," or "intuition" for this kind of experience, which is not rational or irrational but immediate. Some explain it by saying they have received guidance from God.

CHAPTER VIII

The Goal of Growth

What is the point of it—all this hard, endless effort towards further development in oneself? In ordinary life one does not make an effort without a clear purpose, but now that the world may end with a bang any day, and now that scientists are claiming not only that they will be able to create life in a test-tube but to condition the character of life as they will, why bother to try and change ourselves? It was different when people believed, and Browning could declare

> God's in His Heaven
> All's right with the world.

But now that the astronomers and space travelers between them have banished Heaven along with the God who was alleged to dwell therein, why not content ourselves, while we can, with the things that give pleasure—a faster motorcycle, a larger airplane?

That will be the answer for some, despite the biblical warning of Luke *(XII, 20 N.E.B.):*

> God said to him, "You fool, this very night you must surrender your life; you have made your money; who will get it now?" That is how it is with the man who amasses wealth for himself and remains a pauper in the sight of God.

The nobler mind of the humanist makes the advancement of knowledge and service to humanity in the here and now his goal. The religionist does the same but believes—or at least entertains the possibility—that there is meaning in it all beyond our present grasp.

In an allegory called *Gabriel and the Creatures,* Gerald Heard centers his teaching of evolution to children around the theme that further advance for man is now possible only if he will remain generalized, sensitive, open, courageous and growing.

He puts the teaching into the form of a dialogue between the archangel Gabriel and the little mammals who may have been our ancestors. These rather defenceless little creatures at times felt frightened and became querulous about their apparently static and unchanging condition. They felt themselves to be nobodies compared with the great lords of the forest, sward and river whom they admired. To their cries of fearful complaint, Gabriel's voice would answer, "Hang on! Hang on! Believe me, you are still on the main line and they are all off the tracks."

The mammals would answer back, "But tell us then where we're going and what the end is to be. What are we to become?"

The archangel's great light became flushed like a sunset topaz with his deep concern for them. "Please, please don't ask that. Only go on believing, go on trusting, go on being open, sensitive, kind, wondering. Believe me, the end will be far more wonderful than you could ever guess."

"But it hurts," they said, "hurts like hell. We just can't go on unless you tell us why we should always just keep going on, hanging on, plodding on, on, on like this!"

Gabriel gave another glimpse of his glory as he shot up at a beautiful angle, as when a lightning flash springs out from the earth and stabs the sky. The little mammals looked around. "Well, I suppose we'd better just keep on waiting and trying," someone said at last, rather ruminatively. "I guess," he added, "there may be more in the land than you'd think and perhaps more in us than we feel. But what?"

"Heavens," said one making off, "I'd rather live well and then die. I'd rather be strong just for once than go on for aeon by aeon in this sort of fossil-rat condition, a creature that can neither live nor die." And he loped off. Those who remained could hardly stand it, but they ambled along for another million of years and miles, exploring space and time and still not really sure they were getting anywhere.

Not really sure that they were getting anywhere—that is the condition of many twentieth-century human mammals, perhaps of the majority. It has been called "failure of nerve," but some degree of doubt is inevitable in minds that are growing and learning to think independently. It is not wrong to doubt; it is only wrong to give up the struggle before we should. No one should judge another concerning the timing of that moment, for no one knows what is the limit of endurance of another, but "those who can, must."

According to the record, these small, insignificant mammals carried on for a hundred million years before they achieved a full breakthrough into the Cenozoic, so it surely behooves us not to be too impatient or greedy for precise answers. We have an awful lot of growing to do yet before we could understand the full meaning of life even if we were told it. In the meantime, the immediate goal of growth is more *being*, and that is only attainable through more *becoming*.

The watchword of the Zen Buddhists is the brief and explicit "Go on." Go on in the faith that more light will come through as we travel, bringing increasing assurance that the way is valid and does not end in a mirage but in an enlarged state of consciousness that will see "all things new." Most people at some time in their lives have seen the flash of Gabriel's wings, have experienced one of those rare moments when that "deeper and vaster world comes through into consciousness" in some form. The frequency of the contact depends on our readiness to receive.

"Whenever I felt something was basically right," said Dr. Martin Luther King, "whenever I made a commitment to a moral ideal, I felt a cosmic companionship."

This would seem to corroborate Whitehead's words that "right action is treasured in the nature of things," and Huxley's statement that "Our moral principles are not just a whistling in the dark; not just the *Ipse Dixit* of an isolated humanity, but are by the nature of things related to the rest of reality."

That is the goal for this particular stage of the journey; to become ever more securely related to that reality which is, as we say, "out of this world," out of the bounds of our normal apprehension, transcending space and time and the realm of things normally accessible to our limited faculties.

The achievement of such relatedness is a lifelong process, and we should therefore abandon our childish demands for immediate and complete answers and explicit statements about matters doctrinal or eschatological. These are not what come first in the religious life. What does come first is faith in the of watchful, strenuous constancy of habit, that the pinions of the hard Promethean—yet joyous—way that it involves. Only so can new insight take place, new life be experienced, or the significance of rebirth be understood. As the great mystic Plotinus taught, "It is only as the result of long preparation, of watchful, strenuous constancy of habit, that the pinions of your soul will have power to still the untamed body ... and the inner eye will begin to exercise its clear and solemn vision."

Among the last words of Aldous Huxley are these quoted by his wife in *The Timeless Moment:* "What is man for? ... As an act of faith, and I think it is an act of faith shared by most people who are concerned with human decency and liberty, I believe that man is here for the purpose of realizing as much as possible of his desirable potentialities within a stable yet elastic society."

Only as he does so will he be able to glimpse the larger life that gives meaning to this one.

PART II

Meaning Through Religion

CHAPTER IX

Some Contemporary Interpretations of Religion in Different Frames of Reference

Religion only became significant to me when it ceased to be a form of organized belief and engaged my spirit, as the art of his choice engages the artist. . . .
HUGH I'ANSON FAUSSET, *The Flame and the Light*

The word "religion," like the word "God," is ambiguous. It connotes different meanings for different people. One thoroughgoing rationalist, Margaret Knight, speaks of it as "a diseased appendix which ought to be removed," explaining that she uses the analogy of an appendix because, unlike a cancer, "it is a residual organ which once had a function but which now is at best useless and at worst harmful."

At the other extreme, a famous philosopher, Sarvepalli Radakrishnan, holds that "there is no future for man apart from the religious dimension." Could it be that these two highly intelligent people are talking about different things?

Many people, especially in the Western world, regard religion as a matter of belief in a certain system of theological doctrines. The trouble about such doctrines is that their adherents, when of limited knowledge and oversuggestible to authority, tend to suppose themselves to be in possession not merely of a ray of light but of the whole of truth. Their church is "the one true fold," its canon is closed, and there is nothing more to be discussed. They have narrowed down the universe to the limits of their own understanding.

This attitude obtains whether the groupings be "sacred" or "secular," whether it be some branch of puritanism versus catholicism or of collectivism versus individualism. Always the sectarian, as the Rishis said long ago, "believes that all truth is contained in his own little pool."

In view of the ambiguity attaching to the word, it would be wise to distinguish at least between "*a*" *religion* which consists of a system of doctrinal beliefs to be believed, and *religion as inner experience of the ineffable,* known as mysticism. In addition it should be stressed that it is possible to have a religious attitude to life without having a religion, as illustrated in the *Forsyte Saga* when Michael Mont says to his wife, Fleur: "I'm not a believer, so I suppose I have no religion."

True religion does not require us to believe; it requires us to become: it is not a set of propositions to be accepted: it is a state of being to be attained. Therefore in his unselfishness and his sensitivity and concern for the feelings of others, the young man was in fact more *religious* than many a staunch believer. The history of the Christian Church forces us to the conclusion that belief has no necessary connection with religion in its deep and inward sense, for firm belief has all too often been coexistent with ugly intolerance and unspeakable cruelty.

What, then, is inner religion, as distinct from the religion of credal beliefs said to be so "necessary unto salvation"? The philosopher-theologian Paul Tillich gives one answer. He says: "Being religious means seeking passionately the meaning of our existence and being willing to receive answers even if the answers hurt. . . . It is the state of being concerned about one's own being and being universally." That is one quality of religion in depth and inwardness; there are others, such as being sensitive and responsive to the spiritual values of beauty, truth and love; being capable of wonder, awe, and a sense of the holy; being willing to grow and if need be to suffer in the process of inner growth toward one's highest potential, one's true self or soul.

Krishnamurti tells us: "First of all, a religious man is a man who is alone—not lonely, you understand, but alone, with no theories or dogmas, no opinion, no background."

But being alone is not enough: there must be the capacity to listen and to meditate. Religion, as Whitehead says, "is what a man DOES with his solitude." Some can do nothing because they are untrained in silent thinking. "The very word 'meditation' makes my mind go blank." Yet there is nothing obscure about the word. It merely means thinking in depth about the things that matter instead of letting one's mind drift along like flotsam among surface irrelevancies.

To think deeply and purposefully is a form of high prayer, as distinct from petitionary low prayer. Solitude will never spell loneliness or boredom to the man who has learned to think deeply and creatively, but even "retirement" can be a prison of boredom to those who have never found a center of motivation within themselves. Work is better, however mechanical, in that it at least gives the sense of being of some use: and to feel that one is of use is a basic need in man.

It speaks sadly of our schools and training colleges—both theological and secular—that they can turn out people who may be very learned and yet come to feel:

> We are the hollow men
> We are the stuffed men.
>
> T. S. Eliot

And it is equally sad that churches are still more concerned with doctrine than with religion in depth and so produce among many independent minds atheists, agnostics, or at best "light half believers" who can see no connection between what they are told to believe and the problems with which life faces them.

Hitherto, in the West, religion has been largely identified with some form of Christianity. This varies from an immature salvationism, with its crude doctrine of atonement for sin, to the deep wisdom of a von Hügel or a Berdyaev. Some minds need the concrete and the personal, but the so-called average man needs a philosophic religion, which transcends particular "isms" and labels but which includes both the discoveries of modern science *and* the spiritual experience of the inner life.

The essentials of true religion were taught by the prophet Jesus: love of one's fellows, and growth of the seed of God within so that rebirth becomes possible; and with it the awareness of other dimensions of being as described by the modern philosopher Alfred North Whitehead. "Religion ... is the vision of something which stands within, behind and beyond the passing flux of immediate things; something which is real, yet waiting to be realized; something which is a remote possibility yet the greatest of all present facts; something which gives meaning to all that passes, and yet eludes apprehension; something whose possession is the final good and yet is beyond all reach."

But if this "something" was completely beyond all reach and completely eluded apprehension, then it would be foolish to try to talk about it. The mystic is the one who knows that it can be realized, however dimly. As Francis Thompson puts it, in "The Kingdom of God":

> O world invisible, we view thee,
> O world intangible, we touch thee.

Or, if we want Biblical authority, there are the words of Paul: "Faith ... makes us certain of realities *we do not see.* ... By faith we perceive that the universe was fashioned by the word of God so that the visible came forth from the invisible." (*Hebrews XI,* 1–3, *N.E.B.*)

Whether we speak of this Unknown as God, Reality, or the World Invisible is of secondary importance. The difference between the religious man and the materialist is that the latter believes only in the world he can handle and measure. He may at the same time be a humanist, concerned with the welfare of humanity, in which case he will be to that extent "religious," but he will have no use for such "unscientific" concepts as mysticism. Yet many great scientists are mystics. Einstein, for example, asserts that "The most beautiful emotion we can experience is the mystical. It is the sower of all true art and science. [It is] to know that that which is impenetrable to us really exists. ... This knowledge, this feeling, is at the center of all true religiousness."

In other words, the highest form of religion we can know is mystic experience, or what has also been called Cosmic Consciousness, Satori, Nirvana or Illumination. The value of the experience is not merely that it transports the individual into a state of ecstasy—drugs can do that. Its religious significance lies in the conviction it gives of something more; something of which we are infinitesimal but inherent parts and in which we "live and move and have our being."

Speaking on behalf of mystics in general, Evelyn Underhill says: "their evidence of the world they see is no less real than that which is expounded by the youngest and most promising demonstrator of a physio-chemical universe." In *Mysticism,* she asks the skeptic, "Is your world of experience so well and logically founded that you dare make of it a standard? Philosophy tells you that it is founded on nothing better than the reports of your sensory apparatus and the traditional concepts of the race. Certainly it is imperfect, probably it is illusion; in any event it never touches the foundation of things."

The varieties of stimulus leading to mystic experience, as well as the varieties of content, have been most carefully studied and documented by scholars of unimpeachable integrity, including C. H. Spurgeon, M. Laski, and R. M. Bucke.

As an illustration coming from a modern scientist, C. P. Snow tells in *The Search* of the unique experience that overcame him when a scientific prediction had been verified after a series of failures. "Then I was carried beyond pleasure. I have tried to show something of the high moments that science gave to me. . . . But this was different from any of them, different altogether, different in kind. It was further from myself. My own triumph and delight and success were there, but they seemed insignificant beside this tranquil ecstasy. . . . I had never known that such a moment could exist. . . . Since then I have never quite regained it. But one effect will stay with me as long as I live; once, when I was young I used to sneer at the mystics who have described the experience of being at one with God and part of the unity of things. After that afternoon, I did not want to laugh again; for though I should have interpreted the experience differently, I thought I knew what they meant."

A second and different account comes from the autobiography

of the writer and poet Richard Church, *Over the Bridge*. In this case the stimulus, or "trigger," was a verse from the Fourth Gospel which he came upon while he sat "turning the dreary-looking pages of the school edition of the Bible. 'In the beginning was the Word, and the Word was with God, and the Word was God.'"

The result was dramatic in the extreme. "I felt the hair on my head tingling, and a curtain of red blood appeared to fall before my eyes. I leaned forward, clasping myself close, while the world rocked around me. And as this earthquake subsided, I saw a new skyline defined. It was a landscape in which words and objects were fused. All was one, with the Word as verbal reality brought to material life by Mind, by man. It was therefore the very obvious, tangible presence of the Creator."

Even the skeptic who would jib at the word "creator" must admit that the experience points to something outside our normal experience.

The writer continues, "Sitting in the Surrey Lane School... I received a philosophy which I have never lost, a working faith in the oneness of all life.... Everything was now contained for me in the power of the Word."

Mystic or cosmic consciousness is closely related to what is now called paraconsciousness in that both induce awareness of something beyond that which we normally know through our limited senses. There is no need to think of this "something more" as supernatural in the sense of being different in kind; as a beyond which can be known only after death. If everything in life is related, we cannot make such hard-and-fast distinctions. Vaughan's symbolic poem

> My soul there is a country
> Far beyond the stars.

is not meant to be taken literally as referring to some location in outer space, but rather to the psychological distance we have to travel within ourselves, the growth we have to accomplish before we are able to "see" *that* which is always there, "within, behind and beyond the passing flux of immediate things." As we now are, we resemble the rudimentary insects whose horizon ends with the edge of the leaf on which they feed and function.

Extrasensory Perception

The concept of a Beyond applies to every plane of being, physical, mental and spiritual. But while to the mystic it brings spiritual insight that human language is inadequate to describe, psychic experience, or ESP, has now been accepted as a proper study for research by orthodox scientific method. Of this field of the paranormal, or extrasensory, perception, in *The Divine Flame* Sir Alister Hardy has expressed his belief that "psychical research, when it has gone much further, will have a profound contribution to make to man's view of the place of his mind in the universe."

The validity of the phenomena under investigation, such as telepathy, precognition, and hypnotism, has been confirmed by distinguished scientists, but for some obscure reason the narrow-minded scientist or materialist will not look at the evidence. This is not very sensible, for if the universe is open-ended, we should be open-minded to all possibilities still awaiting exploration, even if it is painful to give up some of our earlier ideas. The remark of the boy looking through his microscope, "There are things in life one could not know about," will always be true, because the more we know, the more we realize we do not know. It is well to remember that in the past both religious and scientific systems of thought have often shown themselves too small and too rigid to assimilate new knowledge.

Religion and Evolution

For those who cannot accept doctrinal religion and who regard both mysticism and paranormal psychology as nothing but expressions of wishful dreaming, but who yet cannot be content with a humanism that limits itself to the here-and-now and ignores man's hunger for meaning, is there anything left?

Yes, there is the study of natural science itself. This, as has been said, reveals wonders that can turn some scientists of insight and imagination into mystics. Cosmology, biology and physics have all combined to demonstrate that a very extraordinary thing has happened in the long history of this planet, just as extraordinary as was the discovery that the earth is global and revolves around the sun. This new thing is so wonderful that it is almost impossible to regard it as meaningless.

We have said that the mystic experience is always accompanied by a sense of wonder. It can be aroused by contemplation of "the meanest flower that grows" or by the philosophic realization that we are part of the great organic whole in which everything is related and everything is in a continuous state of change. The contemplation of the evolutionary process arouses a similar sense of wonder. The most "incredible" incident in the whole stupendous process is that, as Loren Eiseley puts it in *The Immense Journey*, bits of stardust once broke off from the sun and, after billions of years, turned into "a two-legged creature in a straw hat" who, by some inscrutable mystery, developed the power to turn around and study the process by which he came to be. This same creature also learned how to observe stars a thousand light years away and to discover events that happened ten million years ago. Fantastic as it sounds, we cannot ignore Julian Huxley's evidence of what a bit of stardust can become:

> Here is a mass of a few kilograms, of substance that is indivisibly one (both its matter and spirit), by nature and by origin with the rest of the universe, which can weigh the sun and measure light's speed, which can harness the tides and organize the electric forces of matter to its profit, which is not content with huts or shelters, but must build Chartres or the Parthenon; which can transform sexual desire into the love of a Dante for his Beatrice; which can not only be raised to ineffable heights at the sight of natural beauty or find thoughts "too deep for tears" in a common flower, but can create new realms and even heavens of its own through music, poetry and art, to which it may be translated, albeit temporarily, from this practical world; which is never content with the actual, and lives not by bread alone; which is always not only surmounting what it thought were the limitations of its nature, but, in individual and social development alike, transcending its own nature and emerging in newness of achievement.

Religion Without Revelation

That of course is man at his highest reaches; we know only too well what he can be at his lowest; seemingly worse at times than primitive savages whom he may elect to despise because he is unaware of the savage in himself. Vast knowledge of techniques for mastering the external world, or worlds, will avail nothing in the future — indeed, there may be no future — unless man can also acquire techniques for learning to know and to sublimate his own dangerous impulses of aggression, malice and greed. We can take hope from the fact that scientific psychologists are themselves now claiming that, as well as all that was once subsumed under the phrase "original sin," we have also within us a "Divine Flame" or upward reach, what theologians call "God Immanent" and friends the "Inner Light." Could we become aware of this, we too would doubtless feel translated with awe and wonder as was the philosopher Kant when he reflected on the starry heavens above him and the moral law within; by which he meant the organically, not the legalistically, moral.

It is experiences such as these that provide a basis for faith in life and a powerful motive for fulfilling our "cosmic duty," for they foreshadow other realms of being than the world as it is known to us through our limited senses.

Introductory Remarks to Chapters X, XI, XII

The Father incomprehensible, the Son incomprehensible: and the Holy Ghost incomprehensible.
From the Creed of St Athanasius

There are many examples of trinities in life, from the clover leaf to the abstract spiritual values of beauty, truth and good. The Christian tradition has long been accustomed to the division of the godhead into three, but there is nothing sacrosanct about this tripartite grouping, and since the Catholic Church has recently announced the doctrine of the Assumption of the Blessed Virgin Mary, "Mother of God," presumably we now have a Quaternity, which recognizes that the female principle is of equal divinity with the male.

It is in the nature of the human mind to try to differentiate the many forces and principles at work in the universe. It also seems inevitable that we begin by assigning personality to them. This is harmless so long as we understand what we are doing and are able to perceive that behind all the gods of the pantheons lies fuller truth; that just as the colors of the rainbow are caused by the diffraction of white light, so all gods and goddesses are but early and partial expressions of the single, all-embracing truth of the Creative Force or Spirit. Keats was feeling his way toward this ultimate unity in the words:

> Beauty is truth, truth beauty — that is all
> Ye know on earth, and all ye need to know.

So was Walter Pater, who said, "All beauty is in the long run only fineness of truth."

This is too abstract for most people who can only imagine God as a person. But assigning personality to spiritual values also creates problems. There is, for example, the story told by Cardinal Cushing of a workman who had been mortally wounded. A priest was sent for, and he began his ministrations by asking: "Do you believe in God the Father? Do you believe in God the Son? And do you believe in God the Holy Ghost?"

The man looked at those around him and murmured: "Here am I dying and he asks me riddles."

The best known expression of the "riddle" is that of St Athanasius, "The Father is God; the Son is God; and the Holy Ghost is God. And yet there are not three Gods but one God." That creed is still part of church liturgy and seems to satisfy the orthodox mind although it contradicts everything that it says as fast as it says it. Peter Abelard at his trial was charged with saying that there is only one God but three ways of looking at him: God the Father, Power; God the Son, Wisdom; God the Holy Ghost, Love. But why only three? Surely there is also God in the Mother, Sister, Brother, Child, not to mention God in the tree, the lily and the snowflake.

> I come in little things
> Saith the Lord:
> Yea! on the glancing wings
> Of eager birds, the softly pattering feet
> Of furred and gentle beasts. . . .
> In brown bright eyes
> That peep from out the brake, I stand confest.
> On every nest
> Where feathery Patience is content to brood
> And leaves her pleasure for the high emprize
> Of motherhood——
> There doth my Godhead rest.
>
> Evelyn Underhill, *Immanence*

Alberic, the accuser at Abelard's trial, avoided difficulty for himself by maintaining that "theology is to be believed, not to be discussed." Abelard, however, possessed a fine brain, which he could not help using. It would be well if these words of his were applied to all theological doctrines, not only the Trinity. He wrote: "And concerning the mystery of the Trinity, we make no promise to teach the final truth, which neither we nor any mortal can know, but at best some likeness of it, some neighbor to it in human reason.... And so whatever we may set forth concerning this most high philosophy, we declare it to be a shadow, not the truth."

It is in that spirit of tentativeness that the following three chapters are written.

CHAPTER X

The Great Hypothesis: God the Father

Such as men themselves are, such will God himself seem to them to be.
JOHN SMITH, Cambridge Platonist

I cannot but say that I believe that some day our conception of God will have become independent of nearly all that has come into it from the primitive Jewish tribal and other pagan conceptions of God which have passed into Christianity, and that our conception will be constantly renewed and growing from all human knowledge and experience from all science, philosophy and psychology.
CANON J. M. WILSON, *The Modern Churchman*, 1924

Changing Concepts of God

It is related that when the Marquis de Laplace, the astronomer, was confronted by Napoleon's criticism of his book *La Mechanique Celeste*, "You have not mentioned God," he replied, "I had no need of that hypothesis." He did not mean that he had no religious faith, for that was not the case. He was in fact referring to Newton's concept of God as the Great Watchmaker who had wound things up and then left them to run by themselves. Newton saw the universe as a mechanism, not an organism.

Many people today are experiencing serious doubt about the official theological concept of God as "a supreme being," a doubt evidenced by the astonishing flow of books and articles under such titles as *Does God Exist? Is God Necessary? Have We Outgrown God? The Future of God, The Meaning of the Death of God,* and so on.

That serious people should ask such questions and express their doubts openly and without fear of social ostracism or any other form of punishment indicates a great advance in tolerance.

Not so many years ago an atheist or even an agnostic was generally spoken of as if he were a kind of moral leper, when his only crime was thinking for himself. But while this newly won freedom is definitely a good thing, it must be stressed that too sudden a loss of one's "Heavenly Father" can be as serious a trauma to the sensitive as the death of an earthly parent. It can also cause moral collapse in the shallow mind which, having found no inner sanction for good behavior, argues, "If God is dead, everything is allowed: let us eat and drink, for tomorrow we die."

What, then, is to be done? It would be damaging to intellectual integrity to try to persuade people back to the concept of "the Loving Father" when they can no longer envisage such a being but feel, rather, with Professor MacTaggart, author of *Some Dogmas of Religion:* "If omnipotent, then not good; if good, then not omnipotent."

A Jewish theologian, Rabbi R. L. Rubenstein, Professor at the University of Pittsburgh, wrote, "After Auschwitz, I find I must reject a transcendent God entirely. God is where we come from and where we go, but he is just not involved in the world in any way."

Another writer speaking of his grim experiences in *The Frozen North* says, "I am a Catholic but I have not been in church for the last five years. . . . I have no religion, because it was of no use to me up North. When I am living up there in that far-off corner of the world, and see how terrible Nature is at close quarters, I come to the conclusion that we all originate from earth and water. Even the Eskimo points to the icy rocks around him and says, 'That is your God who created you.'"

This kind of honesty should not be bypassed or ignored by official religion, for a loving Father-God who cannot be found in the concentration camp or the Frozen North will eventually disappear also from the secure and sunny lands. And indeed there are theologians boldly admitting this. The Reverend Gregor Smith, a British divinity school professor, says: "I can accept without any qualm what we are now calling the disappearance of God from the world. I understand that to mean . . . that God is no longer an object or a phenomenon in the world alongside other objects. . . . I have found no God in the world; he is absent."

The position of Bishop John A. Robinson looks even more bewildering and untenable to many people. When challenged by Ved Mehta that his statement "Man has no longer need of the God hypothesis" did not square with his insistence that "There is a God nevertheless," the Bishop replied, "I believe in both; perhaps I am schizophrenic!"

Since the Bishop is of sound mind, and since it is not possible both to believe and disbelieve in the same God, the obvious explanation is that the God in whom he does believe is not the same as the God he has discarded. And this is as it should be. A schoolboy, once asked by his teacher what he thought God was like, replied, "A snooper."

Outgrowing the anthropomorphic God

What has happened is not, as many people think, that the Bishop is now some sort of atheist, but that his thinking has carried him further and toward more mature concepts. What Rilke meant by the line, "Thou growest with my maturity," was not that God changes but that as our thinking deepens, our thoughts of "God" will change. Winifred Gill tells of how, when she was a little girl, her father said to her, "Every now and again we should revise our idea of God. . . . To worship anything less than the highest that we can conceive is the greatest disloyalty." She adds, "It was a great relief to me when he said that." One can well imagine why. Little children are often deeply disturbed by the strange behavior of their allegedly loving and omnipotent Father who knows when even a sparrow falls to the ground and yet allows the cat to eat it.

According to Freud, the ordinary man cannot imagine God in any other form save that of a greatly exalted Father, "For only such a One could understand the needs of the sons of men or be softened by their prayers, or placated by their signs of remorse." The statement needs modification. Many "ordinary" people are capable of growing toward more conceptual levels of understanding if they are helped to do so.

The late Archbishop William Temple was once taking a Confirmation Service in the course of which he told the candidates that God wanted them to do this and that. Asked afterwards by a friend for his idea of God, he replied: "The source of all spiritual values in the universe," and then he added, "But you would not expect me to talk to these young people in such abstract terms?"

Perhaps not at a confirmation service, but at some time and place it should be done; otherwise many of them will join the ranks of the atheists, and one will continue to hear the complaint that "They tend to drop away after confirmation."

It is here that current religious teaching shows itself lacking in the sort of elementary educational psychology that is applied to other subjects. As a general rule no help is given to enable the child (or adult) to make the transition from one concept of God to another, with the result that when the early concept is questioned or discarded, a vacuum is left.

The kind of growth to be encouraged is illustrated in the case of seven-year-old Ursula, who was distressed over the terrible directive given by Jehovah to an old father: "Take now thy son, thine only son Isaac whom thou lovest, and offer him up as a burnt offering."

When she was asked to think whether a really good God would give such an order, her face cleared and she exclaimed, "Oh, I see! God didn't really want Abraham to offer up his son; Abraham only *thought* he did."

The history of the world might have been very different if more people had learnt to make that distinction instead of using the Bible as a fetish and quoting all its words as divinely inspired. The Jews, for example, might have asked themselves, "Did God really choose us as his favorite people, or was that only wishful thinking on our part?"—as is clearly the case when Americans say, "God has blessed America and will continue to do so," or when Britons sing, "God who made thee mighty, make thee mightier yet."

How to Prevent Later Unlearning
A good teacher is always fostering this growth process.

"I used to think God was a sort of big Man in the sky," remarked a seven-year-old.

"And what do you think now?" Pause.

"He's a spirit."

"What does spirit mean?"

"Something you can't see."

"Can a thing be real if you can't see it?"

Eventually answers came in from the class; yes, the wind, electricity, sound-waves, myself, love, etc. The deduction was made that although one could not see these things, one could experience their effects, so they must be real, and therefore spirit might be real in the same sort of way—that is as an invisible power making for beauty, love and truth. It was suggested that we kept a lookout to see if we could ever observe this power at work in ourselves.

That at least was a start in stimulating thought and making the transition from God as a person to God as a power; not necessarily omnipotent, since there were other powers too, pulling in an opposite direction, and these sometimes triumphed. It also initiated the process of looking into one's self to try to find out something of what went on there. The children became almost "scientifically" frank about themselves. "I know I like to show off; that's my weakness," said Graham.

"And I like to make you think I know the answer when I really don't," piped up another.

This is "religious" education at ground level, and without it no theological superstructure will do much good nor the word "spirit" ever have much meaning.

Stages in Changing Ideas of God

Another very helpful way of enabling people to stretch their minds and think more flexibly about God would be to tell them something of man's changing thoughts about "him" through the ages. The history of ideas and of how they have originated, developed, and been outgrown by new ideas gives ground for hope that still better ideas will evolve in the future to bring new faith and hope and enterprise into the hearts of men everywhere. Starting from sun worship and idol worship, the teacher would pass on to anthropomorphic gods in the physical and mental form of man, sometimes even coming down to earth and intermarrying with humans.

Next would come the anthropopathic stage, in which the gods were no longer conceived in the bodily form of man but still had man's mental, emotional and spiritual attributes and behaved much as man himself would like to behave.

Between polytheism and monotheism came henotheism, a stage in which there were still gods but one was regarded as superior to all others and as "the only true god" — as the Old Testament prophet Elijah determined to demonstrate once and for all in the dramatic trial with the worshippers of the god Baal *(I Kings, XVIII)*. The story is a vivid one if presented in its psychohistorical setting. Unfortunately, Bible readings from the church lectern are presented as factual truth and God is always regarded as the same God, no matter whether he is giving savage orders to Samuel, *(I Samuel, XV, iii)* or showing mercy and loving kindness in renewing the widow's oil-cruse *(I Kings, XVII, xiv)*.

In short, every stage of God's development (which is really our own development) can be found in the Bible, from the vengeful anthropopathic being of the Second Commandment to the being described by the greatest of all mystics who taught that "the kingdom of God is within" and that it was possible for man to be in union with God when he had found his true self or soul, when he too would be able to say, "I and the Father are one."

Recognition of Ignorance
Before going on to discuss the significance of God immanent it is necessary to remind ourselves of our great limitations, of the embryonic stage of our development, and of the fact that we are at present overloaded with brain at the expense of sympathy, imagination and intuitive insight. We are therefore ill equipped to know more than a very little of the nature of ultimate reality, which is far beyond the comprehension of even the wisest of men.

We are in the same situation as Newton, who said of his discoveries that they were but a small pebble on the shore, while the great ocean of truth stretched out before him. Truth is stretched out before and around us all, but we can only take therefrom as much as we are mentally and spiritually equipped to apprehend.

It was a wise father who, in reply to his little girl's impatient "Why do you not answer my question?" said gently, "Because there are so many, many things I do not know, Judy." He was giving his child something more important than the information she wanted, namely a beginning of humility in the face of ignorance.

Could we but realize the extent of that ignorance, there would be less place for dispute between the religious sects. For this reason Meister Eckhart challenged people of the twelfth century: "Why dost thou prate about God? Almost everything thou sayest about him is untrue."

Much later, Matthew Arnold made the same protest: "We do not deny conscious intelligence to God. . . . All we say is that men do not know enough about the Eternal not ourselves that makes for righteouseess to warrant This either a Person or a Thing. We say that no one has discovered the nature of God to be personal or is entitled to assert that God has conscious intelligence. Theologians do assert this and make it their basis for religion. . . . We object to their professing more than can be known."

However not all theologians are guilty of making unwarranted assertions. Canon Streeter would have agreed with Matthew Arnold. He said, "The grandest of all follies is to imagine that any words we use or any definition we can frame about God and his dealings with men CAN HAVE THAT KIND OF EQUIVALENCE TO THE REALITY which alone could make them premises for a valid logical deduction."

The Inductive Approach

If, then, a personal God cannot be known as the conclusion of a syllogism because there is no major premise from which we can deduce "His" existence, can inductive logic be more helpful?

The answer is yes. Those who cannot believe in a God on the authority of church or book can find their own truth, whatever name they may give to it, by building on their own experience. The name is unimportant, as is illustrated in this vivid little story: When Zabolgi was asked "Who told you what you know of God?" he replied, "Told? Whoever is so stupid that they have got to be told about God? Never did any man know God from *tolds;* you get God by *feels.* All the told there is to it is his name.

You call him God; I call him Gala. I English Gala's name so you can understand me."

It is indeed the *feels* that register, not the indoctrination with words. Of what use is it to *tell* a child God loves him and he ought to love God if he has had no experience of love? The Archbishop of Canterbury recommended the inductive approach in a radio talk. After speaking of the supreme things in the universe that call forth man's wonder, reverence and love, he continued: "How exciting this is. Without using the word "God," or any of the old images of God, we are thinking about man's response to the highest and best that he knows, and his reverence for the highest and best as being the meaning of the universe. . . . It is in the sense of love, goodness and self-sacrifice, which is the stuff of which belief in God is really made."

The humanist would agree thus far. "It is a fact," writes Julian Huxley, in *Essays of a Humanist,* "that many phenomena are charged with some sort of magic or compulsive power and do introduce us to a realm beyond our ordinary experience. Such events and such experience merit a special designation. For want of a better, I use the word 'divine'. . . . The divine is what man finds worthy of adoration, that which compels his awe. . . . Though gods and God in any meaningful sense seem destined to disappear, the stuff of divinity out of which they have grown and developed remains."

Not all scientists agree with Sir Julian's use of the word "divine" or with his statement that the study of the evolutionary process can "introduce us to a realm beyond our ordinary experience." That is too bad for them, for these experiences are not a matter for argument.

Of Sir Julian's grandfather, the great Thomas Henry Huxley, biographer Ronald W. Clarke writes: "It became clearer as the years passed that his influence as a scientist lay in the fact that he was very much more than a scientist. . . . He knew, not so much by reasoning but intuitively, that some things were not merely beyond the breadth of human intelligence but were of a nature that put them outside the scope of man's mental measuring instruments. . . . He never ceased feeling the wonder of the universe; his astonishment at its mysteries never grew less."

To experience wonder, a sense of mystery, of something beyond the world we ordinarily know, something ineffable to which we instinctively apply the word holy or sacred, is to have a religious attitude to life. Indeed Plato went so far as to say: "By wonder we are saved."

Thus far prelate and humanist are at one. Where they part is over the question of a personal God. Doctor Ramsey goes on to say that he bases his belief on "an intuition of faith that this reality (the highest and best that we know) is no less personal than we are." Perhaps not, but the word "personal" as applied to an omnipotent, omniscient being must mean something very different from our human use of the term. And having candidly admitted that "God is beyond our understanding" why does he also say that "The old images are still . . . true and valid. The images of God the Creator, God the King, God the Father, God the Judge, as well as God within us." If God is "beyond our understanding," how can we make all these positive assertions about him?—unless they are intended to be taken as symbol-words for the highest we know, in which case the list would seem strangely inadequate.

God Immanent in Man and in Nature
Moreover such images are dangerous in that they suggest that God is a King, Judge, Father, dwelling somewhere *outside* his creation. The Archbishop does add, as if in afterthought, "as well as God within us." The phrase "God within us" seems pretty meaningless, if not blasphemous, to most people, although, since Jesus himself was responsible for it, it is necessarily part of Christian doctrine. How can we possibly know God within ourselves? Bianco da Siena of the fifteenth century gives the answer in indirect yet definite terms. Of the *amor santo,* the divine love, he says:

> For none can guess its grace,
> Till he becomes the place
> Wherein the Holy Spirit makes his dwelling.
>
> *Songs of Praise,* Hymn number 217.

So once again, knowledge of truth is a function of being and of becoming. Like can only be known by like. Only as we become more like what we profess to admire can its grace be in us. William Blake put it simply:

Where mercy, love and pity dwell
There God is dwelling too.

He also said, "Why stand we here trembling around, calling on God for help, and not on ourselves in whom God dwells?"

But the mystic feels God to be not only in himself but in all creation. In the words of Alfred North Whitehead, "God is in the world or nowhere, creating continually in us and around us. This creative principle is everywhere, in animate and in so-called inanimate matter, in the ether, water, earth and human hearts. This creation is a continuing process, and the process itself is the actuality, since no sooner do you arrive than you start on a fresh journey. In so far as man partakes of this creative process does he partake of the divine, of God; and that participation is his immortality." (Dialogues.)

Another scholar-mystic, Evelyn Underhill, has expressed the same truth in Mysticism: "I cannot feel that life comes from Another, from One who is qualitatively external to all that lives and grows. On the contrary, I feel this whole world to be moved from the inside, and from an inside so deep that it is my inside as well, more truly 'I' than my surface consciousness."

In his book The Way and Its Power Arthur Waley tells us that to the Chinese artist of the past God was not a monarch standing outside his creation, as the carpenter stands outside his artifact, but was the hidden way and power that is in the flow and course of Nature. As is shown in their paintings, the Chinese found images for this hidden away in water and wind, in air and sky. Jesus, also an artist, found it in the grain of mustard seed which a man took and sowed in his garden, where it grew to be a tree; in the yeast which a woman took and mixed with half a hundred-weight of flour till it was all leavened. Are not these more suitable images and signs of "God" than monarch, judge, king?

All artists are mystics in some degree in so far as they see a little further into life and its meaning than does the pedestrian literalist; but the greatest of all the arts, the art of living, is the most neglected. Working at such arts as music, movement, painting, and drama is good and eminently desirable but not enough to save mankind from disaster, unless we are also working at making our own lives into works of art and using the power of the upward reach (the God within) to conquer the power of the downward pull which is also within us.

This is what the ancient Chinese sage Lao-tzu meant when he said we can only know the way of the Spirit by traveling it:

> When one looks at it, one cannot see it:
> When one listens for it, one cannot hear it;
> However, when one uses it, it is inexhaustible.

It is also what the seventeenth-century mystic Angelus Silesius meant by the poem containing this verse:

> In me is God a fire
> And I in him its glow;
> In common is our life,
> Apart we cannot grow.

It would seem that the Chinese artists and the American Indians were once, and perhaps are still, better able to think in these terms than are the Christians of the West, in spite of the teaching of their Master. The Indian felt that he belonged to the land and was its son, not that the land belonged to him. Writing of the Iroquois, D. J. Hall says, "They pass through the land silently, leaving as little trace as sunlight through wind. . . . The land is their food, their drink, their religion and their life. Their songs and their prayers are all of the earth, the sky and the rain."

Another student of the native Americans, Mary Austen, tells, in *Can Prayer Be Answered?* how Tinnemaha, the medicine-man of the Paiute tribe, explained to her that Indians do not pray to a god but to a principle existing in all created life, accessible to man, responsive to him, workable. He called this principle "the friend of the soul of man," something alive and kindly, but not personal. . . . He made the most interesting point that prayer to Him or It was not a matter of asking but of doing. You had to reach Him or It through a motion in the soul.

Relationship

We need a third pronoun, but failing that, "thou" is a more living term than "it." "Thou" suggests a relationship, and it is the felt relationship that matters, not the word used. "In the beginning is relation," says Martin Buber, in *I and Thou,* and it is a great tragedy that industrial civilization is cutting us off ever more rapidly from relationship with the earth, our mother; especially tragic that fewer children are able to know the joy of close contact with her, and so many miss this groundwork for genuine religious education. It is a serious spiritual deprivation, but not of course so serious as the deprivation of human relations.

An infant deserted by its mother and parked in an orphanage may not die physically, but unless he can form a love relationship with someone, neither will he grow inwardly and become his potential self. Love is a kind of cement that unites individuals and saves them from being so many isolated and useless "bricks." "I" become through my relation to the "thou." The infant's first "thou" is his mother, of whom he was so recently an organic part. He has no "I" apart from her and cannot at first distinguish between her body and his own. Her warm breast is probably more like part of himself than are his own toes. Separation is inevitable, but it should be very gradual in the early stages, or new relationships to new "thous" will not be formed and growth toward maturity and independence will not take place. But with normal development the individual will come to depend less and less on either earthly or heavenly parents as he finds the relationship between his own spirit and the Spirit of the Universe, the eternal "thou." Failing this, he joins the "Wilderness of the Lost." He is like a branch severed from the tree that gave him life.

There are many of these "orphans in the universe" today who feel rudderless in a meaningless world because they have never learned to make the transition from God as Father to God as Spirit. This is in large part the fault of their teachers, who have fed them with words rather than with experiences and have stressed the importance of belief rather than of growth.

We can now see why the question "Do you believe in God?" is the wrong kind of question, as the word "God" has no precise connotation, its significance varying with the individual's stage of development. Many people, after long searching, will come to agree with James Weldon Johnson, who wrote: "I do not know if there is a personal God. I do not know how I can know. . . . What does matter, I believe, is how I deal with myself and how I deal with my fellows. I feel that I can practice a conduct towards myself and my fellows that will constitute a basis for an adequate religion, a religion that in the midst of joy, pain, frustration and bewilderment may yet comprehend spirituality and beauty and serene happiness."

That briefly sums up the situation of the religious-minded agnostics who wisely follow the teaching of the Buddha to "look into the works of creation, rather than try to interview the Creator himself." What they find will vary according to temperament, interests and ability to see.

A class of school children once sent a telegram to Einstein, which ran as follows: "Do you believe in God. Stop. Prepaid reply fifty words."

The answer was neither "yes" nor "no" but "I believe in Spinoza's God who concerns himself with the harmony of all being; not in a God who concerns himself with the fate and actions of men."

Katherine Whitehorn, author of *Keep It Brief,* writes: "When my brother was at school he sent home a card marked 'URGENT' which said, 'If no God, what about moral imperative?' and got back a telegram saying 'God is moral imperative in long beard and trousers.' Shook his housemaster quite a bit! This was one way of bridging the gap between anthropomorphism and abstract concepts."

The harmony to be found through the study of higher mathematics could be the way of only the very few. More obvious and intelligible to many would be the wonder of the evolutionary process. Irene Orgel has written an amusing fantasy in the form of a dialogue between God and Jonah, which illustrates this wonder. Jonah is struggling to make a difficult advance in his thinking:

> "But before man," asked Jonah, shocked out of his wits, "do you mean you understood nothing at all? Didn't you exist?"
>
> "Certainly," said God patiently, "I have told you how I exploded

in the stars. Then I drifted for aeons in clouds of inchoate gas. As matter stabilized, I acquired the knowledge of valency. When matter cooled, I lay sleeping in the insentient rocks. After that I floated fecund in the unconscious seaweed upon the faces of the deep. Later I existed in the stretching paw of the tiger and the blinking eye of the owl. Each form of knowledge led to the more developed next. Organic matter led to sentience which led to consciousness which led inevitably to my divinity."

"And shall I never call you father any more, and shall I never hear you call me son again?" asked Jonah.

"You may call me," said God agreeably, "anything you please. Would you like to discuss semantics?"

Whatever view we may hold about the details of the evolutionary process and of the means whereby it came about, the fact will always remain that, somehow or other, it has come about thus far, and that its direction has been forward; that a man is a finer creature than an amoeba, a gazelle than a jellyfish. Moreover, an imaginative study of the process does three things for us. It gives us the basis for a natural theology in that the world now begins to seem more like an organism than a mechanism; it gives a basis for morality in causing us to feel that it is our manifest duty to carry the process forward; and it gives a new sense of life's meaningfulness in the realization that we ourselves are part of this mighty cosmic process. "So Jonah found himself alone on the road to Nineveh. And yet he was not alone. He knew that he was a man who had come out of the sea. And he knew that he was a man who had come out of the sun. And in Nineveh he took root, and he flowered in the expression of his consciousness until he died." He had achieved relationship.

At this point someone will surely say, "That is all very well, but what about the evil and horror in the world? What have you to say to that?" I think the only thing to be said is that we recognize and accept it but we cannot yet understand it.

The Hindus were honest in conceiving their God Shiva as both Creator and Destroyer, and one Old Testament writer makes his god say, "I the Lord, create evil." But these frank recognitions of evil do not explain its existence, and we cannot agree with Browning's dismissal: "The evil is null, is naught, is silence employing sound."

We may derive some comfort from the doctrine of bipolarity in all things, which makes each quality of life necessary to its opposite. As Jung puts it: "Light has need of darkness, otherwise it could not be seen as light." That is true, but is it also true that evil is necessary to good, sorrow to happiness, cowardice to courage, hate to love? Sometimes it seems so. Certainly our lives are a continuous struggle or tightrope-balancing between the two alternatives; a little too far in the wrong direction and we may crash.

We must accept our ignorance. Meanwhile we may be thankful that we can at least see our direction and can know that more light will dawn as we follow it.

CHAPTER XI

Jesus as Prototype

Without the emergence of superior or differently adapted individuals—beneficial mutations in other words—the doorways to prolonged survival of the species would . . . be closed.
LOREN EISELEY, *The Mind as Nature*

The implication of the above words is that it is a good thing for the race that men are created unequal. Only so can we learn from each other and avoid a dead level of changeless mediocrity. We are all agreed that there should be equality of opportunity and equality of justice before the law, but without variation of native endowment in such things as intelligence, intuition, and capacity for love and courage, there would perhaps be little progress. An individual can, of course, be superior in one quality and at the same time inferior in another, can be brilliantly clever but lacking in human warmth.

Biologically speaking, a mutation is a change resulting in the production of a new species. Was Jesus one such "beneficial mutation"—was the difference between him and other men so great that it came to be regarded as a difference in kind? Or was he, as the Church teaches, "Very God of Very God," invading our planet from somewhere outside it, "sent down from Heaven"?

It has become increasingly difficult to believe the latter, and it is more than doubtful that he himself believed it. He does seem to have wondered if he was not a Messiah of the inner life, not an external deliverer.

When faced with the charge of blasphemy, he quoted the words of the Psalmist: "I have said, 'Ye are gods; and all of you are the children of the Most High.'" (*Psalm* 82, 6.) He asked his accusers, "If he then called them gods, how can you say I blaspheme when I call myself the Son of God?" (*John X*, 35.)

The implication was that "if every man who has anything of God in him is 'a child of God,' obviously that applies to me too"; or as the Epistle to the Romans has it, "All who are led by the spirit of God are the children of God." (*Romans VIII*, 17.) But poetic or figurative language was evidently wasted on Caiaphas the High Priest.

That thoughtful Christians are themselves beginning to entertain the idea that Jesus was a godlike man rather than a man-like god is evidenced by the words of Barbara Ward, a liberal Roman Catholic:

> It seems to me that the Eastern idea that the highest aim of man is to achieve unity with a higher consciousness, to move to new levels of freedom by breaking away from the constraining egoisms of the self, can, at this point, be fruitfully confronted with the great Christian doctrine of the second Adam—the doctrine that Christ is the firstborn of a new race of men.... Here surely we have a clue to our future.... If what we seek is a new type of life, which expands human consciousness, takes man beyond his present level of intelligence and raises him to new heights of creativeness and capacity, we have to look for it in the great leaders of the world's religions, and above all, in Christ himself.

Interplay of East and West
This passage puts forward for consideration a quite different interpretation of the man Jesus from that normally presented by "orthodox" Christianity, an interpretation more in line with evolutionary thinking and more interested in the future than in the past, in what man can become than with his "sins and wickednesses," which burden him with a sense of guilt and cause him to feel the need of a Messiah or Savior whose death will atone for sin. This does not mean she ignores the evil in man or dismisses it as unimportant—who could do that today?—but that like Jesus and the Buddha, she places the emphasis on the possibilities for development that lie within him. She suggests that if we would learn how to break away from our "constraining egoisms" we too could create or achieve union with the higher consciousness latent within ourselves, as stressed by the great

Eastern religions, and so bring into being "a new race of men," of whom Jesus might be regarded as the firstborn.

Whether he was the firstborn, or *primus inter pares,* or merely one among other Mahatmas, who can say? In *The Quest of the Historical Jesus,* Dr Albert Schweitzer tells us, "The Jesus of theology is not alive for us, being bound hand and foot with the graveclothes of dogma." In any case we have no exact techniques for measuring the quality of being. What matters is that we should recognize his stature and understand the deep meaning of his teaching. For what made Jesus great was not the theologies men have constructed about him but the depth of his insight into the meaning and purpose of life and the completeness of his dedication to that purpose. It could be that such an integrated selfhood and such a high level of spiritual maturity produced healing powers and knowledge of occult forces greater than had ever previously been known, this resulting in the kind of "mutation" to which Barbara Ward refers. One can entertain such a hypothesis without making it into a dogma that must be believed, and without deifying the possessor of such powers. Those who "protest too much" about the truth of their dogma are more likely to sow doubt than belief in the minds of their hearers.

Deification of the unusual was a not-uncommon tendency in the past. Believers in the anthropomorphic gods of ancient Greece and Rome found no difficulty in the idea of their gods' appearing on earth. "When the people of Lystra saw what Paul had done [in curing the cripple], they lifted up their voices saying: 'The gods are come down to us in the likeness of men' . . . and they called Barnabas Jupiter and Paul Mercury." *(Acts XIV, 11.)*

The psychological need to find someone to worship as super-human and the tendency to be unduly impressed by unusual power are also evident in the habit of ascribing divinity to emperors and ruling monarchs. Charles I had to pay heavily for his acceptance of the doctrine that because kings ruled by divine appointment they could do no wrong. The hypostasizing tendency extends to things and theories as well as to persons. The "divinely inspired" Bible is still treated by many people as a fetish; and the party doctrine of the totalitarian is held to be above all criticism. To indulge in original, creative thinking can still be a dangerous occupation, leading to punishment or death. Even as late as the seventeenth century, Oxford undergraduates who questioned the authority of Aristotle were fined five shillings.

All such extolling of what is mine: my beliefs—my political party, my country, my religion—arises largely from a love of power and self-glorification, rather than from a love of truth. For the thirty years from 1618 to 1648, Catholics and Protestants slaughtered one another until they were reduced to cannibalism, in the attempt of each to make his own concept of religious truth dominant in Europe. Today the same strong passion to be right and to impose one's viewpoint on others still exists. But it is in process of changing its direction from religious to political beliefs.

At the Council of Nicaea it was a matter of vital importance whether Jesus was pronounced to be *homo ousia* or *homo iousia*. There is only one 'Ιωτα different in the spelling, but once the decision was taken in favor of the former, it would have been unwise, if not dangerous, to disagree. Now that the matter is once again up for discussion, distinguished theologians are openly expressing different viewpoints with a freedom from fear hitherto unknown. For example, the Rev. H. A. Williams, ex-Dean of Trinity College, Cambridge, writes: "Christians claim that Jesus was God. As a matter of metaphysics this is impossible to understand; so considered, it may even be meaningless. But behind the statement of the doctrine lies something we can understand as absolutely real. *Jesus is the vision of man fully himself.* And man fully himself shares the life of the Creator. . . . What is a Father but he whose nature I share?"

Bishop Robinson stresses the same point when he says: "Unless he is really one of us, unless he is the truth about our humanity, the Gospel just cannot get started. The majority of men today cannot even hear what Jesus represents because it appears so unlike their normal experiences."

So, according to these and other religious specialists, the truth about Jesus is not that he was God's *only* begotten Son sent "down" into the world to suffer torture and hideous death as a vicarious sacrifice for the sins of mankind. What sort of God would require such a terrible thing? He was not a human god but a godlike human. He was *kyros* but not *theos*; Lord but not God. He gave but one commandment: "Thou shalt love." He formulated no doctrines that must be believed and he never asked to be worshipped as God. It is certainly more encouraging to poor, struggling humanity to envisage him as human, as manhood at its highest level. Viewed this way, his life, like the lives of all great men, decreases our pessimism about human nature by revealing its magnificent possibilities and showing that the depths of evil to which man can sink may be outmatched by the heights to which he can attain.

Unless creeds and doctrines can be shown to have an inner significance that relates to our human condition, there is little point in retaining them. As Alan Watts writes of the Incarnation: "There can only be redemption for the human race . . . if the incarnation of God in the man Jesus is representative of God in every man, as Adam represents Lucifer in every man. Yet, with rare exceptions, the theologians insist that the godhead is incarnate in one man only, the historical Jesus. This confinement of the Incarnation to a unique event in the historical *past* thus renders the myth 'dead' and ineffective for the *present*. For when the myth is confused with history, it ceases to apply to man's inner life." *(Myth and Ritual in Christianity.)* In other words, if we are going to talk about Incarnation at all, we must recognize it wherever it is to be found, in both the world without and the world within, for, as William Temple once said, "Unless all existence is a medium of revelation, no particular revelation is possible." It is all God's world, and if God exists, "He" pervades all creation, including man, His presence being more conspicuous in some than in others.

Many people, however, feel this is no answer to the alleged statement of Jesus "I and my Father are one." The words were not, of course, recorded at the time, as John's Gospel was not written until some seventy years after the death of Jesus and is recognized by historians as the interpretation of a mystic rather than a verbatim record of his life and teaching. Mystics have frequently described their experience as "union with God," meaning at-one-ment rather than identity with the ultimate reality, the spirit of the universe. Jesus was one of the world's great mystics, perhaps the greatest, not primarily because of his teaching but because he had broken through into the dimension of spirit and appears to have lived his brief life entirely in that dimension, receiving his inspiration from it.

His fate was not unique. The Sufi Al Hallaj was also condemned for saying, "I am the Truth." Dr K. Walker writes in *The Conscious Mind:* "If he had been allowed to explain what he really meant by these words, he would probably have answered as Jacob Boehme did — that it was not he himself who was speaking but an inspired voice within him. But Al Hallaj was never allowed to defend himself, and he was crucified in the city of Baghdad in A.D. 922."

Jesus was invited to explain himself to the High Priests but evidently felt the attempt would be hopeless, since they were "without understanding."

The teaching he gave, and perhaps the "miracles" he performed, naturally resulted from his sure knowledge of the "Higher Worlds" (or "God"), but the teaching was not new. "There is no such thing," writes British theologian Dr N. Micklem, "as a specifically Christian ethic; the requirements of love and mercy, of gentleness and of thoughtfulness, have been stressed often before in man's spiritual history. It was no new teaching that the love of God and man was the summing-up of the law of God. Perhaps he and he only is that which is new in Christianity." (*British Weekly.*)

In what sense "new"? It looks as if Catholic and nonconformist are agreed that some kind of fundamental change had taken place due to a heightened spiritual consciousness. But this can only be regarded as a difference in degree from other men. Otherwise Jesus would hardly have made that hopeful forecast: "The works that I do shall he do also," or have rejected the title of "Good Master." (*Matthew XIX,* 17: "There is none good but one, that is God." *A.V.* and "Good? . . . one alone is good." *N.E.B.*)

When that other Master in Israel secretly asked what his teaching was all about, he was told in effect that it was about growth and becoming, to fit oneself for rebirth into the spirit dimension. (*John III,* 6. "You ought not to be astonished when I tell you that you must be born over again." *N.E.B.*)

Similarly Socrates at his trial had tried to explain himself and his life's work, for which he was also condemned to death (though by a more humane method than that of the Romans or any other civilization). In immortal words he testified, "For I do nothing but go about persuading you all, young and old alike, not to take thought for your persons or your properties, but first and chiefly to care for the great improvement of the soul."

Earlier still, Gautama the Buddha, walking by the Ganges, was asked, "What is thy teaching, O Lord?"

He replied, "To know the self and control the self; and he who can conquer the self is better than he who rules over a great army"—which was another way of saying the same thing, for the lower self must be controlled in order to make way for the true self, overself, or what Jesus called the soul.

The word "soul" might be defined as that aspect of the psyche which is responsive to spiritual values. In our own day the Spanish philosopher Unamuno has made it clear that the soul is not a separate entity, readymade at birth. He says, "We are not born into this world with souls; we are here in order that we may win souls." This was also the "Gospel" of Jesus.

To achieve that goal of a higher spiritual consciousness, it is necessary to continue the growth process, not by mechanically and superficially following another, but by thinking and learning for ourselves. Jung asks, "Are we to understand the imitation of Christ in the sense that we should copy his life ... or in the deeper sense that we are to live our own proper lives as truly as he lived his? It is no easy matter to live a life that is modeled on Christ's but it is unspeakably harder to live one's own life as truly as Christ lived his." That is to say it is easier, in the sense of being more straightforward, to copy another, than to find out for oneself who one is and what one has to do. To become one's own true self is both difficult and complex. It means building up our minds, our selves, from earliest infancy when consciousness barely exists save in the form of a few confused sensations, to the end of life when, if faithful to the task, we shall have brought sufficient order, harmony and purpose into the "buzzing confusion" to have earned some degree of personality or soul.

We sometimes hear it said of one, "He is a real person,"

meaning that he has coherence and a center from which he functions. He knows his direction even if the goal is as yet unseen. Of another we hear the comment, "He is all in pieces," or "all over the place." To be thus dispersed is to have failed to find one's true self or center and to be at the mercy of every wind that blows. Obviously Jesus was right in saying that to win the whole world materially would profit such a man nothing. Indeed many who even win the pools become more than ever uncertain as to who they are and what they ought to become, as do many modern young with their extra time and money.

Dietrich Bonhoeffer said that God is trying to make us into men, which is another way of saying that our destiny is to grow and become mature persons. No one can do this for us, not even by dying on a cross. Jesus tried to make this clear to his disciples, telling them, "It is expedient that I go away." Otherwise they would always rely on him instead of trusting to the power of the Spirit within themselves and growing in cooperation with it, their true center.

What, then, is Christianity? Baron von Hügel said there were five Christianities; but with the gradual fading of religious persecution and authoritarianism, people have been free to think independently about their beliefs, with the result that we now have a large variety of thought systems all calling themselves Christian. There are theologians of distinction like Bultmann who advocate demythologizing Christianity, and fundamentalists like Jehovah's Witnesses and Christadelphians, who cling to what they are convinced is the very truth of the Bible. There are scholars like Geikie Cobb or Alan Watts who would retain the mythos as *symbolic* truth and seek to unravel its deeper meaning where that exists; and there are revivalists like Billy Graham who offer instant salvation on the literal acceptance of John III, 16.

All this is inevitable in view of the numerous differences in both temperament and intelligence among men, and it is desirable that each should be free to follow his own way of belief and worship. What is undesirable is that any should claim to have found all truth and should insist that his interpretation is the only right one.

In the last resort there is only one distinction of importance, that between the "Christianity" of Jesus and the "Christianities" that have been built up about him. It is surely the first that should have authority, but throughout the centuries it is the second with which men have concerned themselves. Whole libraries of volumes have been written on such theological matters as the Virgin Birth, the Messiah, the Incarnation, Atonement, Resurrection, Ascension, Second Coming and the rest, none of which can be regarded as of fundamental importance to religion itself, since as many good and intelligent people disbelieve as believe them. The danger of giving them priority, sometimes to the extent of saying that "an error in doctrine is worse than an error in life," is that the institution making such a claim comes to regard itself and its particular doctrines as of more importance than the teachings of its Master:

> The vision of Christ that thou dost see
> Is my vision's greatest enemy.
> William Blake

The doctrines of the established churches tend to be regarded as static and final, with the result that they lose vitality. The teaching of Jesus was essentially evolutionary and concerned with bringing to birth in man a new self of enhanced awareness. This is the pearl of great price, the treasure hid in the field, the leaven in the lump, the seed of the spirit which has been planted in the heart of every man and contains the potentiality of his future selfhood if its growth is rightly fostered. This is the meaning of the phrase "the Kingdom of God within."

The hope and intention of many Christians is that Christianity as now understood shall become a world religion. In its present form this would be impossible, as its doctrinal basis is too small and is unacceptable to many thinkers. It is too small in that it ignores or even denies much important new knowledge, such as evolution. Julian Huxley writes, in *New Bottles for New Wine,* "I believe that, by the time its implications have been properly grasped, the discovery of evolution is destined to have a more revolutionary and more constructive effect upon ideology than any other scientific discovery yet achieved. . . . It is the most powerfully integrative of concepts . . . uniting nebulae and human emotions, life and its environment, religion and material nature, all into a single whole."

If Christianity is not to be as static as Marxist dogma it must shed its outgrown doctrine of atonement and its too narrowly conceived doctrine of incarnation and relate whatever is of eternal validity in the Gospels, such as the emphasis placed on inner growth, to the new knowledge that has been given us.

This "new" knowledge is basically what Jesus himself taught in the Parable of the Sower and all the other parables concerned with inner growth. One of the "new" psychologists, Ira Progoff, expresses this new-old truth as follows:

> As the oak tree lies hidden in the *depths* of the acorn, so the wholeness of human personality with its fullness of spiritual and creative capacities lies hidden in the *depths* of the incomplete human being silently waiting for its opportunity to emerge. The role and purpose of a holistic depth psychology (holistic in the profound, integrative meaning that Jan Christian Smuts gave the term) are to describe the possibilities hidden in the depths of man, to ascertain the processes by which they unfold, and to devise practical procedures with which to expedite and enlarge the natural growth of personality.
>
> *Depth Psychology and the Modern Man*

At this point psychology and Immanentist theology unite in believing that somewhere in the depths or heights of the psyche, there is "a power that worketh in us" *(Ephesians III, 20)* making toward the fulfilment of our inner evolution.

Sometimes a natural scientist joins forces with them, expressing the same insight as Jesus into the affinity between the power-potential in the seed and in the psyche. In *You and the Universe,* Norman J. Berrill writes: "With the expansion of a seed of life . . . new structures, new properties and new functions steadily emerge. . . . Our common unawareness of it is irrelevant. The reality is there—creative development in every individual and creative evolution through the course of the ages." But man's further evolution lies in his own hands and is dependent on his own growth toward ever higher levels of consciousness.

What makes Jesus still of interest and importance is the fact that he knew with certainty that the life we normally know is not the whole, but that within, behind and beyond it there is another ineffable condition or dimension of being which transcends the confines of time and space. He knew it because he had been there; he had won his way through into this knowledge when tempted in the wilderness to follow the lower and cheaper way to power. This conquest and the dedicated commitment that followed it gave him a spiritual power that enabled him — as it has enabled all great seers of the invisible — to act and speak "as one having authority."

What people happen to believe about the metaphysical nature of Jesus will generally be what they have been taught to believe. Only the few can be expected to try to think it all out for themselves. But Christology and theology are of secondary importance. What everyone should take seriously about him is the hard core of his teaching. This is of universal importance because on its acceptance the future evolution of man on this planet depends. The hard core was, and is, that the way onward is the way inward. Only through knowledge of self is self-transformation possible. The outward piety of the Pharisees was severely condemned because "ye make clean the outside of the cup and the platter but your inward part is full of ravening and wickedness" *(John III, 7)*.

This, in varying degrees, is true of all men. Unless we recognize the fact, we shall not understand or accept the basic teaching that it is necessary to evolve, to be reborn. Believing all the creeds and doctrines including the Thirty-nine Articles will not make a person a Christian in any significant sense. "Ye must be born again . . . of the Spirit" is all we know and all we need to know to make the religious life meaningful. Albert Schweitzer has summed up the matter as follows:

> The truth is that it is not Jesus as historically known but Jesus as spiritually risen within men who is significant for our time and can help it. Not the historical Jesus, but the spirit which goes forth from Him and in the spirits of men strives for new influence and rule, is that which overcomes the world.
>
> *The Quest of the Historical Jesus*

Two thousand years ago Jesus did not know what we know today about the evolution of the cosmos and of life on this planet, but his teaching was in accord with the new knowledge. He perceived that man's duty and destiny lay in the growth process, in fulfilling the evolutionary requirement to become new men, equipped to enter a new dimension, the dimension of spirit.

CHAPTER XII

Another Dimension
(God the Holy Ghost)

But the Godhead of the Father, of the Son and of the Holy Ghost, is all one.
The Creed of St Athanasius

The religion of the spirit will be the religion of man when he has come of age.
BERDYAEV

I have often said that there is a power in the soul which neither time nor world can touch. This power proceeds from the soul and belongs to the soul for ever. I have sometimes called this power a fortress, sometimes a light, sometimes a spark in the soul; but now I say it is more than any of these things. . . . I wish to give it a nobler name than any I have yet given it, but it disowns all names. . . .
MEISTER ECKHART

The names and forms that men have given it mean little enough. They are only the leaves and blossoms on the stem of the eternal tree.
CARL JUNG

The Dimension of the Spirit
We have seen that although God, in the theological sense of a supreme person, is no longer credible to many people, those things from which the idea of God arises remain; the beauty of the earth, self-sacrificing love, the creative principle and harmony in life, the all-over trend in evolution, and so on.

These are of course, all to be matched by their polar opposites of hate, ugliness, cruelty and fear, and the horror and terror in Nature itself. If a good God created "All things bright and beautiful," the question must be asked, "Who created the other?" Since the question cannot be answered, it would seem wiser to leave the existence of God as a supreme person an open question for the present, to think instead in terms of the life-process so far as we can understand it, and to explore what grounds for faith may be found therein.

That man was potential in the stardust is a very great wonder, and although it is said that perhaps 99 percent of life's experiments have been failures, yet at least one, with a hominized mammal, has succeeded—thus far. His future is not assured; it may end in self-destruction, for the savagery of his nature is not yet adequately chastened by the power of the spirit of love that also dwells in him.

A dangerous situation has been created by the overdevelopment of the frontal cortex, and it remains to be seen whether the imbalance can be corrected in time. The fight is on, and all who are awake to the real nature of the menace and its challenge should be throwing their weight behind the forces of the spirit in a mighty attempt to help them prevail.

The pessimist, looking only at *human* history, sees it as a repetitious story of wars and cruelty, of man's inhumanity to man. He is partially right, but he is only looking at one small section of man's total history, just as a materialist looks at only one part of all the available data. It must be remembered that less than a million years ago, man had little or no concern for the things of the spirit. He was too "new," and too busily occupied with the bare struggle for existence. Perhaps the remarkable thing is not that he has progressed so little in his half-million years, but that he has begun to care at all for the things of mind and spirit.

We must not be like the mother who said despairingly: "This baby is not growing; he does not walk or talk any better tonight than he did this morning." To get our lives into true perspective we should view them in relation to the entire evolutionary process. Teilhard, amongst others, helps us to do this by showing evolution as a succession of stages in which one sphere of being outgrows and transcends the previous one. He gives us the following brief summary of the many stages of development that have taken place on "this bit of sidereal matter on which we dwell" during the thousands of millions of years of its history:

> The cosmic fragment from which our world emerged has gone through stage after stage of zonal composition, from the barysphere, central and metallic, surrounded by the rocky lithosphere, that in turn is surrounded by the fluid layers of the hydrosphere and the atmosphere . . . four concentric layers. Next came the living membrane of the flora and fauna of the globe, the biosphere.
>
> *Le Phénomène Humaine*

And lastly, with hominization a new stage is in process of becoming, called noögenesis. This means the formation of yet one more layer of membrane, the noösphere, which will spread over and above the biosphere and bring into the story something wholly new. Something as new and different as when fishes learned to breathe in a new element, and even more significant for the destiny of man.

Not that the difference between animal and man is absolute in every respect; a dog can feel affection and anxiety and risk his life for his master; a chimpanzee shows surprising intelligence and ability to give and receive love. Here are the beginnings of the life of the spirit. But man, although deeply rooted in all earlier levels of being which live on in him—mineral, chemical, vegetative, and animal—has crossed a threshold in that he is not only conscious with the simple awareness of the animal, but he is also conscious also of himself, able to turn round and observe himself, to criticize or admire what he sees in himself.

Unfortunately he does not often use this new capacity or test it in action. He is too content to remain at a half-"animal" level and refuse life's challenge of "over to you." For however automatic the process may have been hitherto, no one, not God himself, can take human life any further forward without man's conscious cooperation. That is inevitable because of the nature of the creature man.

"But if he wanted them to be good," asked a little child, "why didn't he make them good?"

Presumably because "he" wanted men and not robots, and a man must have freedom to make mistakes and to grow of his own volition and by his own power toward whatever is his maximum potential in the sphere of mind and spirit. It is still uncertain whether he will use his freedom wisely, whether he will succeed in finding his true self and so fulfil his great promise. At present some do and some do not.

Ibsen says: "Life brushes aside those that will not kindle," i.e. will not respond to the light of the spirit. A hard saying, but the unlit lamp is useless to life's purposes, as Jesus made clear in his parable of the wise and foolish virgins. Where there is no oil the lamp cannot be lit, or, as Lao-tzu said: "Where there is no suitable endowment within, the Tao cannot abide," for it has nothing with which to make contact. God Immanent has been spoken of under various images, such as the inner light, the divine flame, the candle of love that shineth in the soul. But these have to be cultivated; before we can expect to know them we must make a "suitable endowment within."

Why should we make the effort to do so? What explains the compulsion, where it exists, to search for this deeper truth and to make it "the effective power" of one's being? Man's spiritual aspiration is a strange thing and needs explanation, for it is anti-entropic; that is to say, it resists the natural tendency to run down, to take the line of least resistance. It means continuous effort when one might sit back and take the weight off one's feet, so to speak. But it is also true that effort can be enjoyable. I have seen an infant scream with rage when the mother lifted him on to the bench where she wrongly supposed he wanted to be. What he really wanted was the feeling of achievement of having got there by himself.

A young airman, going up into the Battle of Britain for the first time, said to a friend: "Don't pray that I may be kept safe; pray that I may behave well." Why should it matter to him how he behaved? Why was not the instinct of self-preservation stronger in him than his concern to behave well? Is it not because he felt the pressure of the Spirit and because man's further evolution is destined to be in the direction of the psychological and spiritual rather than the biological?

Hitherto strictly academic psychology has tended to ignore the spirit of man as altogether too vague and indefinable a part of his personality for serious consideration. Fortunately, today there are depth psychologists of insight who perceive that there is more to man than instinct and cognition. One of these, Ira Progoff, writes:

> When man has encountered the inner principle working in the psyche, and when he has recognized it as the effective power of his being, the framework of his experience alters and he can perceive the world in a new context. With this he becomes capable of meeting his anxieties and overcoming them by means of a superior inward power.... He has touched the deep psychic fount of creativity within man.
>
> *Depth Psychology and Modern Man*

When in everyday language we say of Mr X that he has a fine spirit, we mean roughly that he is courageous and adventurous, and that he dares to live dangerously in the service of some worthwhile cause; while "a poor-spirited creature" is one lacking in initiative, gives up easily and shows defeatist tendencies about life in general. The former has, whether consciously or not, "encountered the inner principle working in the psyche," which can become "the effective power of his being." This is psychological language for pictorial phrases such as "the Divine Flame," "the Inner Light," "God Immanent" and so on. The defeatist is one who has not found this inner principle and so feels that life is meaningless.

Freud, the great pioneer in one aspect of unconscious life, bypassed the spiritual function in man, finding in him only the instinctive drives. This perhaps is not surprising in view of the fact this his work was mainly with sick, unbalanced minds that were "poor in spirit" in a way not meant in the beatitudes, where this phrase presumably referred to genuine humility.

Not surprising either was his verdict that human beings are "mostly riffraff." Jung felt obliged to part company with him over this matter, for he found that the instinctive drives of greed, aggression, power-lust and the rest were not the whole story. The drives, he said, "are continually colliding with something, and we may as well call that something spirit." He added: "I am far from knowing what spirit is in itself, and am equally far from knowing what instincts are. The one is as mysterious to me as the other. Yet I am unable to dismiss the one by explaining it in terms of the other.... They are terms that we allow to stand for forces whose nature we do not know."*(Modern Man in Search of a Soul.)*

When Freudian psychology first became popularized, it was not uncommon for its more superficial exponents to explain away spiritual or religious interests in terms of unsatisfied sex, at that time regarded as the most important of all motivations. Today it is beginning to be recognized that what is repressed is spirituality more often than sexuality. It is of course as mistaken to "repress" the one as the other—repression meaning in the Freudian sense unconscious forgetting.

Only a complete materialist would deny the spirit of man in such conspicuous instances as the self-sacrificing loyalty to truth of a Giordano Bruno, the passion for justice in a Voltaire, the uncalculating love of her fellows of an Edith Cavell, the Promethean will of a Lloyd Garrison. But neither should it be denied that these qualities of the spirit exist potentially, in however small a degree, in nearly all men, and that they can, if fostered, develop more fully. They must indeed do so, for it is not the nature of life to stand still. If we are not getting better, the chances are that we are getting worse, drifting backwards. This we cannot afford to do, having now acquired too much dangerous knowledge for spiritually immature people to handle.

Thus far we have spoken of the spirit of man. Now the question of major interest arises: Does man's spirit relate to anything beyond itself? Is the divine spark in him the reflection of a larger light which is referred to as the light of the world, or the spirit of the universe? To the unimaginative and narrowly scientific mind which recognizes only measurable fact and observable phenomena, the question is as irrelevant as would be talk of flying in outer air to the grub in its cocoon. But it is possible to fall over backwards in the determination to be "scientific" at all costs, to refuse even to entertain a hypothesis concerning anything which is not amenable to measurement and logical proof. However, there are also scientists who tell us that the truly scientific attitude is openmindedness. The mathematician Herman Weyl says that "the world is being made by modern science to appear more and more an open one. It points to something for which it is a portal." We cannot find that "something" by reason alone, and there are great mathematicians who admit the place of disciplined intuition as a source of knowledge. 'Most of what we think and say with our conscious minds and speech is shallow and superficial," said

Alfred North Whitehead. "Only at rare moments does that deeper and vaster world come through into conscious thought or expression. They are the memorable moments of our lives when we feel, when we know, we are being used as instruments of a greater force than ourselves for purposes higher and wider than our own."

And Whitehead's friend and collaborator the rationalist Bertrand Russell, speaking of mystic experience, says: "I have no wish to deny it, nor even to declare that the insight that reveals it is not a genuine insight. What I wish to maintain — and it is here that the scientific attitude is imperative — is that insight, untested and unsupported, is an insufficient guarantee of truth, in spite of the fact that much of the most important truth is first suggested by its means. . . . Reason is a harmonizing, controlling force, rather than a creative one. Even in the most purely logical realm it is insight that first arrives at what is new."

With guarded caution, Russell also wrote in *Mysticism and Logic,* "I believe that, by sufficient restraint, there is an element of wisdom to be learned from the mystical way of feeling." He omits to say that there is a kind of cognition as well as of feeling in the mystic experience.

The only way in which intuitions can be tested is by constant self-observation to make sure we are not dressing up our unconscious needs and wishes as lofty ideals; and by constant application of our ideals to our living. Perhaps in a very long run science and religion will come together in a realization that truth is one, that religious truth can be tested "scientifically," and scientific truth can be perceived in a religious context. This must indeed be so if, as we are now being told, the world is less akin to a mechanism than to an organism in which there are no isolated facts or parts, but all are so completely interrelated

> That thou canst not stir a flower
> Without troubling of a star.
> Francis Thompson, "Mistress of Vision"

And if everything in life is thus connected, then we are not only "members one of another," affecting and being affected by each other in all we do or say, but we are also members of the whole; not as isolated entities but as cells in a living organism, giving to and receiving from it. As conscious beings, we should find strength and support in this awareness of our relationship to the whole and to the life which permeates it.

Julian Huxley wrote of his brother, in *Aldous Huxley*, "He will go down in history as the greatest humanist of our perplexed era." But he added — and this might surprise some "humanists" — "One of his major occupations was how to achieve union with that 'something deeply interfused' that pervades existence and makes for righteousness, significance, and fulfilment."

So there is no barrier between a humanist and a religious attitude to life, only between humanism and doctrinal religions. For this reason Professor Dewey advocated the use of the adjective "religious" rather than the noun "religion"; for it is possible, as Lord Cecil said of Aldous, to have "a profound sense of some spiritual reality, not to be apprehended by the senses, existing beyond the confines of time and space, serene, inviolate, and ineffable," without believing in any doctrines.

There are other scientific discoveries that will help us toward a nondoctrinal religious approach to life, and to what is called a natural theology. One fact of great interest is that behind the everyday world revealed to us by our senses lies a nonmaterial world. Matter, once regarded as solid and impermeable, and defined as that which has weight and can be measured, is really a form of energy (the splitting of the atom has revealed the nature and possibilities of that energy both for good and ill), and energy is in turn "a manifestation of force fields." The gravitational field is the best known of these because of Newton's experience with the apple and his recognition of its possible connection with the gravitational pull of the planets toward each other.

Kirtley tells us that the primitive fish developed fins to give a sense of balance to the force-potential of the all-pervading gravitational field, and developed light-sensitive epidermic cells in response to the presence of the electromagnetic spectrum. It was said earlier that man's upward reach, his spiritual aspirations, are hard to explain. Kirtley suggests that to account for such aspirations it is not illogical to postulate the presence of a spiritual "field" among the universal fields of force, analogous in some ways to those to which our ancestors responded.

Whether or not the analogy is sound, whether a spiritual forcefield is in any way comparable to a magnetic electrical field, the fact is that many spiritually advanced human beings are aware of the pull of such a force, affecting them in the way that Whitehead has described, acquainting them with the existence of another dimension.

This is why the mystics have to be taken seriously. They have not only felt the magnetic attraction of the "spirit-field" but have glimpsed it. For them the noösphere is not merely a layer of culture of art and learning, but a glory within and beyond the world of the senses. Behind the veil, they "see" a translucent, an "unobstructed, universe." A faint comparison would be that of seeing the Grand Canyon for the first time when one's immediate reaction is: "What am I seeing? It cannot be true." The mystic's vision vanishes perhaps without return, but he has for a moment seen *through* the world of the senses and has discovered that what we normally know of life is not the whole but that a far more wonderful world lies beyond and within it.

Of mystics in general Greta Hort writes, in *Sense and Thought,* "That they know is certain; what they know cannot be told."

It cannot be fully told, but many have tried to say something of their experience. For instance, Father Bede Griffiths has written of what happened to him during his last year at school: "Up to that time I had lived the life of a normal schoolboy, quite content with the world as I found it; now I was suddenly made aware of another world of beauty and mystery such as I had never imagined to exist, except in poetry.... It was not only that my senses were awakened.... Nature began to wear a kind of sacramental character for me.... I approached it with almost religious awe, and in the hush which comes before sunset, I felt again the presence of an unfathomable mystery ... a presence which seemed to be drawing me to itself." (*The Golden String.*)

The last words suggest, like Francis Thompson's symbolic poem "The Hound of Heaven" that something beyond is trying, or waiting, to get through to us as soon as we are qualified to recognize and receive it: that, in Tennyson's words, "spirit with Spirit can meet."

In view of all the evidence, Kirtley is right in saying that among the universal fields of force, it is not illogical to postulate the presence of a spiritual field. It would indeed be illogical not to. But a warning is necessary. We shall get nowhere if we forsake the everyday world in the hope of living continuously in the blissful state called cosmic consciousness, Nirvana or Satori. Life is a test of the truth of the spirit. Life and spirit are two powers or necessities between which man is placed. Spirit gives meaning to his life and the possibility of the greatest development. It is equally true to say that life is necessary to spirit, for spiritual truth is nothing if it cannot live. It must therefore be put to what Sir Alister Hardy and William James call the pragmatic test; that is, whether it works in living.

> Man is a citizen of both time and eternity,
> A swinging wicket set between
> The unseen and the seen.

He has a dual allegiance, and to withdraw from the world permanently in order to dwell "in the spirit" would be as fatal as to suppose that the world can flourish on its own, un-regenerated by the spirit. If spirit is reserved for church rituals or mountain tops and does not function in the Security Council, the Houses of Parliament, the factory, the classroom and the home, it is of no use. For, as the Buddhist monk de-clared while tearing up his scroll:

> The words are all written;
> The words are all read;
> But if we don't LIVE them,
> They'll still be quite dead.

It may be that one known as a "master" works best in the distant mountains, at least for a time, but the masters are rare and what they can do is not possible or desirable for ordinary mortals. We have to try to apply our ideals to the practical problems of living in the everyday world if they are to "cut any ice" with other people or become healthy growing-points in ourselves. A seed must be well planted in the common earth if it is to function properly and bring forth good fruit. A fine skill and balance are required in relating ideals to the difficulties of living. This in turn requires training in self-observation and self-discipline, as all the great religions have taught. It is a high art. The artist with brush or pen shapes raw material into picture or poem in accordance with his vision; even so, the artist in living will bring the insight of his spirit to work in finding creative solutions to the problems with which life faces him, and which are his raw material.

Being born of the spirit implies entry into a new dimension, but unlike the mode of the biosphere, being born into the noösphere is a life-long process. The Greek philosopher and mystic Plotinus described some of the ways by which the desired end of spiritual illumination may be reached, such as "The love of beauty which exalts the poet; that devotion to the One; that ascent of science which makes the ambition of the philosopher, and that love and those prayers by which some devout and ardent soul tends in its moral purity towards perfection."

Many other, more detailed directions for the great highway have been devised, including the various forms of Yoga, but each man must find and follow his own particular path toward realization of his spiritual self, overself or soul, for it is not possible to become mature if always acting under direction. That is why Jesus told his sorrowing disciples, "It is for your good that I am leaving you." (*John XVI*, 7. *N.E.B.*) He wanted them to grow up and learn to think for themselves.

In conclusion, then, we may say that the word "spirit" refers both to an inner force in man and to a sphere of being around and beyond man with which, or with whom, he can make contact, and from which he can draw new life. Psychology should not ignore the spirit of man, for it is as much a reality as his instinctive life. It is a power in his life, weak or strong, urging him to live in accordance with his own best standards and to make fully actual his own highest potential selfhood. The French have condensed the truth of its immanent presence in the brief statement "*Plus est en vous.*"

CHAPTER XIII

Religious Unity in Doctrinal Diversity

One of the major tragedies in the world today is the fact that the great religions, which ought to help unite mankind in mutual understanding and good will, divide mankind instead and add to our humanity's disunion their own special prejudices, animosities and dogmatic fanaticisms.
HARRY EMERSON FOSDICK

In the present state of our knowledge of other spiritual traditions than the Christian, there is no further excuse for religious provincialism. This knowledge is now so extensive that it is becoming hard to see how anyone can be considered theologically competent, in the academic sense, unless thoroughly well-versed in traditions outside the Christian alone.
ALAN W. WATTS, *Myth and Ritual in Christianity*

If what has been said so far has given a fair statement of what religion essentially is—inner growth toward deeper understanding and higher levels of spiritual consciousness that reveal new meaning—then there should be no place for disputes among the varied systems of belief, no place for proselytizing, still less for assertions about the superiority of one's own system of beliefs.

The important and interesting difference between two people will not depend on what each happens to believe but on their stage of maturity. A Dean Inge or Bishop Barnes would have far more in common with Aurobindo or Shankara than with many of the Christians of his own church. The reality of the difference is not between one creed and another; it is between a religious or a materialistic attitude to life, between maturity and immaturity of being. As the mystic Evelyn Underhill clearly saw: "To those who keep their eyes on 'the one thing needful,' denominations, creeds, ceremonies, the conclusions of philosophy . . . are matters of comparative indifference. They represent merely the different angles from which the soul may approach that simple union with Brahma, which is its goal, and are useful only insofar as they contribute to this consummation."

Alan Watts has observed that "when Christian theologians become subtle and mystical, and sometimes when pressed to say in conversation what they really mean, it becomes increasingly difficult to tell the difference between Christianity and, say, Vedanta." Vedanta is one of the oldest religious philosophies in the world, a system of spiritual disciplines and techniques of meditation which help the individual towards a closer relation with reality, the unknown, Brahma—what the Christian would call "union with God."

Just as it does with the ancient Eastern religion of Vedanta, Christianity at its best also finds common ground with the Indians of the West, as illustrated by the meeting of two American students of religion. Dr. David McAllister wrote of his talks with Mary Cabot Wheelwright: "We both rejoiced in the chance to talk Navajo and talk religion. She, a Unitarian, and I, a Quaker, found it natural to join in a reverent appreciation of the beauty and depth of Navajo religious poetry, literature, philosophy and art. The mystical, transcendental quality of Navajo religion spoke to us strongly because of our own religious backgrounds." In her study of the Navajo religion, Mary Wheelwright said she had discovered a content lofty enough to be taken seriously by all civilized people and advanced enough to enrich the thinking of all Christians.

That Christians could possibly have anything to learn from American Indians or from Eastern Indians will appear as a shocking suggestion to the orthodox. Yet that distinguished student of religion Dr Kenneth Walker wrote in *So Great a Mystery,* "I can only state that my own Christian beliefs have been immensely strengthened by the study of the Vedas and the Upanishads."

Why then do we impoverish ourselves by refusing to look at more than one expression of truth or one interpretation of life?

When we insist on "One church, one faith, one Lord," we oppose the diversity that is inherent in the nature of things. Spiritual truth alone has universality; no particular set of beliefs can be exclusively and finally true at this rudimentary stage of man's development. Moreover, the great inequalities between men, and the wide variations of insight and temperament, necessitate equally wide variations of expression. A uniformity of belief and ritual would lead to something as dull and barren in religion as it would if imposed on the field of art, music or literature.

We learn through our differences as well as through our similarities. It is unnecessary, therefore, for the Christian churches to flagellate themselves for what they regard as the "sin" of diversity, for where there is a kindly and generous spirit there will be toleration of differences. It is possible and indeed desirable to have diversity without exclusiveness. "Sin" lies in the lack of such tolerance, in the determination to impose one's own viewpoint, in the indifference to and lack of interest in the viewpoint of other people, and in the unexamined assumption of superiority.

Some religious beliefs and forms of expression are obviously more advanced and perceptive than others, some are more living and growing than others; but so far as the world's great religions are concerned, a mature person who has not only studied them from the outside but lived with them, as Gandhi lived with Christianity, will find much common ground between them. Gandhi remained a Hindu, but not in any narrow sense. "My Hinduism," he said, "is not sectarian. It includes all that I know to be best in Islam, Christianity, Buddhism and Zoroastrianism .... Truth is my religion."

Likewise, Tagore, speaking of the religions of which he had deep knowledge, wrote: "I rejoice when I find that the best in the world have their fundamental agreement." No one questions the integrity or the spiritual stature of these two men. Would it not be wise, therefore, to pay some attention to their outlook, to start putting the emphasis on the fundamental agreements, to build together on our affinities instead of trying to proselytize?

If only Christians had learned to outgrow totalitarianism in their outlook and expressions, it is possible that the political totalitarianism from which we are suffering today might not have come into being. If peoples had been trained by their various pastors to show interest in and try to understand each other's viewpoints, it is possible that such training might have carried over into the ideologies of politicians. But while the vast majority of Christians still indulge in "theological imperialism" and treat the Bible as the only inspired source of wisdom, why should they expect Marxists to be more flexible or show more humility than themselves?

The Christians' claim that theirs is the ultimate religion for the human race is often profoundly offensive to religious non-Christians.

An American Indian told Jung that he saw the white man as the Aryan bird of prey with an insatiable lust to lord it over every land — and with a megalomania which leads one to suppose that Christianity is the only truth and the white Christ the only Redeemer.

Edward Conze, puzzled by the reluctance of Buddhist friends in Ceylon to discuss religion, was given this explanation by one of them: "These Christians are quite impossible people. Very soon after we meet them they will tell us that 'God is Love.' This means nothing to us, and we say so. Thereupon they inform us that Christianity teaches a particularly sublime kind of 'love' which we Buddhists do not understand and in which we are sadly deficient. We will bear this for a time, but when they persist in boasting about their own wonderful kind of 'love,' we feel at last constrained to point out that our own Buddhist 'love,' imperfect though it may be, has never yet included the burning of witches and heretics, the massacre of infidels, or crusades and that kind of thing. Thereupon the fat is in the fire, and we are treated to a dissertation on the difference between 'true' and 'actual' Christianity, which just takes our breath away. In fact, the sum total of human benevolence is rarely furthered by such disputations."

As Dr Conze comments, "There can be no game of cards if someone holds all the trumps." And there can be no discussion if someone "knows" all the answers and is therefore not interested in hearing his opponent's point of view and discovering where it might coincide with his own. This is a pity, for there is a great deal of common ground between Buddhism and Christianity.

John Coast, author of *The Railroad of Death*, tells of how during nearly three years of imprisonment a Thai named Boon Pong risked his life smuggling in medicines and money to prisoners, "not out of political conviction but out of Buddhist charity." How does Christian charity differ from or improve upon Buddhist charity?

> It is not too much to say that almost the whole of the moral teaching of the Gospels, as distinct from the dogmatic teaching, will be found in Buddhist writings, several centuries older than the Gospels. For instance, of all moral doctrines collected together in the so-called Sermon on the Mount, those which can be separated from the theistic dogmas there maintained are found again in the Pitakas. In both religions we find the same exhortation to boundless and indiscriminate giving, the same hatred of pretense, the same regard paid to the spirit as above the letter of the law, the same importance attached to purity, humility, meekness, gentleness, truth and love. And the coincidence is not only in the matter; it extends to the manner also in which the doctrines are put forward. Like the Christ, the Buddha was wont to teach in parables and to use homely figures of speech, and many of the sayings attributed to him are strangely like some of those found in the New Testament.
>
> *Journal of the Pali Text Society*, 1923, pp. 43–44.

This last is a fact ignored by most Christians. How is it that this remarkable identity in the teaching of the great masters is almost completely overlooked? Presumably because what is taught as Christianity is often something quite different from what Jesus taught. The "Christianity" he taught was concerned with the expression of universal truth and is therefore acceptable to the thoughtful Buddhist, Jew, Sufi or Humanist. It is the religion of all who are wise and good. But the "Christianity" that has been built up *about* Jesus is something different. In order to be a Church Christian, one must not only believe that Jesus is the one and only *logos* or Word of God but must also, officially at least—and as expressed in the church hymns and liturgy—believe in an omnipotent and loving God who yet required appeasement by the tortured death of his only son before he could forgive mankind. Literalists will find biblical sanction for this belief:

> For if the blood of bulls and goats sanctifieth . . .
> How much more shall the blood of Christ. . . .
>
> *Hebrews IX,* 13/14.

What Jesus himself taught was a different and universal truth: the necessity of rebirth into the realm of spiritual consciousness, of becoming new men. Recently the Buddhist U Thant has said the same. "More of us will have to get to be a new kind of man — universal man."

Psychological Hindrances to Religious Unity

The provincialism that keeps us in deplorable ignorance of other religions is caused largely by two emotional factors. One is the love of feeling superior.

Whether or not we agree with psychologist Alfred Adler that the urge to be right, superior and powerful is the most compelling urge in human nature, we must at least agree that the urge is a very strong one, for we can observe it everywhere, within us and around, from the kindergarten child singing "I'm the king of the castle" to Alexander the Great sighing for more worlds to conquer; from those who believe in themselves as "God's chosen people," whether Jews or Aryans, to those who believe in "My country, right or wrong." In the saint who wrote "Love suffereth long and is kind" there was a less respectable urge which declared: "As we have said before, so say I now again: if any man preaches unto you any gospel other than that which ye have received, let him be accursed." [*Galatians I,* 9.]

The early Saul found it as difficult to tolerate those who dared to differ from him as did Philip of Spain, who, when implored to mitigate the barbaric cruelties of the Inquisition, replied, "I will not have God insulted by wrong belief."

The other emotional factor that hinders religious maturity is fear, the unconscious and understandable fear of the narrowly educated that if there is truth in other religions, then their own cannot be the sole container of truth. That is something that could not be faced, and so it is safer to ignore the others and take note only of their defects.

Such an outlook results from a pitifully limited and altogether inadequate religious education. We should teach the young to be primarily concerned with truth, not with "my" truth. It is both dishonest and dangerous to teach Christianity or any other religion as if it unquestionably embodies the whole of truth— dishonest because in fact there are many wise and good men who do not believe this; dangerous, because the practice defeats its own ends and paves the way toward later doubt and a turning away from all religion. It is dangerous also because,

> Like any other form of imperialism, theological imperialism is a menace to permanent world peace. The reign of violence will never come to an end until, first, most human beings accept the same true philosophy of life; and until, second, this perennial philosophy is recognized as the highest common factor to all the world religions.... If these conditions are not fulfilled, no amount of political planning, no economic blueprints however ingeniously drawn, can prevent the recrudescence of war and revolution.
>
> Aldous Huxley, *The Perennial Philosophy*

Politically speaking, "imperialism" has become a dirty word in the democracies, but Christian imperialism lives on, and many churches are more concerned with the horizontal extension of their boundaries and the size of their congregations than with religion in depth. The totalitarianism of most missionary hymns, such as

> Jesus shall reign where'er the sun
> Doth his successive journeys run
> His kingdom stretch from shore to shore
> Till moons shall wax and wane no more.

is reminiscent of the delight one felt as a child in seeing so much of the world painted red. Unfortunately, religious totalitarianism receives its imprimatur from the "Holy Bible," which makes such assertions as: "There is no salvation in any one else at all, for there is no other name under heaven granted to men, by which we may receive salvation" *(Acts IV,* 12)—a truly shocking statement.

The terrible things that have been done in the name of the Prince of Peace by Christians of every sect should cause humble heart-searching before Christians set out to convert others.

Some of these others are more spiritually advanced than we are. The insights of a Vivekananda, the profundity of an Aurobindo, and the wisdom of a Kabir throw more light on the teachings of Jesus than do the tedious sermons of many "Christians." The latter would serve their Master and serve Christianity better by abandoning the claim to an exclusive knowledge of truth and by reconsidering what Jesus meant by the word "gospel" in his directive to his disciples: "Go ye into all the world and preach the gospel unto every creature." (Mark XVI, 15.) Verses 9 to 16 are in any case thought to be a later interpolation.

This will mean a very difficult change of attitude for those accustomed to thinking in terms of absolutes, but it is not impossible. Since even Rome has begun to modify her traditional image of herself as the one and only true church and has admitted the principle of freedom of conscience, we can dare to hope not only that all Christians will learn to tolerate each other in the unity of the spirit but that they will learn to do the same with peoples of other religions—or of none.

Such a hope is not entirely fantastic, for here and there the thing has already begun to happen, as at the 1958 Dallas Conference when Buddhist, Catholic, Episcopalian, Hindu, Jew, Mohammedan and others met to discuss world problems and their relation to religion. On this occasion there was no disagreement with the statement of the Buddhist that all the great religions had as their foundation the basic concept of the eternal law, an eternal "God" or an eternal power, or with the words of Mr B. K. Nehru:

> Nothing comes more naturally to a Hindu than the belief that in my Father's house are many mansions, that Moses or Jesus or Mohammed is just as much an incarnation of the divine as Rama, or Krishna, or Gautama. The tolerance of Hindus does not mean that there is no difference between the right and the wrong, or that you should not through persuasion and agreement attempt to convert others to the conception of right as you see it. But it does imply refusal to impose . . . and a readiness to seek light from all sources . . . that nobody can have a monopoly of right, and that therefore the manners and customs as well as the morals and modes of thought of others . . . deserve respect and dispassionate consideration.

Owing to his limited and anthropomorphic concept of God, the average Christian tends to dismiss Buddhism as a religion without a god. Yet those who are able to reach wider and deeper levels find common ground, as, for example, the Quakers and Buddhists in Japan who recognize the identity between the inner light of the former and the buddha within each one of us of the latter. "The Quaker conviction of universality has opened the way for Friends to worship with members of other faiths, as well as to work beside them to implement convictions held in common," says Teresina Havens in *Buddhist and Quaker Experiments with Truth*.

If we have "readiness to seek light from all sources," we shall discover that there need be no conflict between one religion and another, for if the goal of all religion is increase of spiritual BEING in ourselves, the way of spiritual BECOMING is fundamentally the same for the Catholic, Methodist, Quaker, Vedantist, Baptist, Buddhist, Moslem, Taoist, Bahaist or Hindu. That is the way of self-transcendence and increase of awareness in the realm of the spirit.

Gautama called the way "the Noble Eightfold Path," and he elaborated it in some detail. Jesus described it in the form of vivid parables, Lao-tzu and the Vedantists in brief epigrammatic statements, others in such poetry as the Bhagavad-Gita.

For all such expressions of the truth, tolerance is not enough. We should feel "reverence for reverence" and seek to enrich our minds through contact with all who have traveled further than ourselves or who are traveling in the same direction but along a different road from ourselves. We can do this without discarding our own "particularities," but we must be willing to lose our attitude of superiority and show more respect for the heritage of others. We need to cultivate a greater willingness to listen and learn, as well as to talk and instruct; to recognize the fact that all true insights are nourished from the same source; to realize that, being such incomplete and fragmentary creatures as we are, our horizons might well be enlarged and our vision deepened through contact with the insights of others belonging to a different tradition.

The Eastern mind — and therefore the Eastern approach to religion — tends, like the mind of Jesus, to be primarily concerned with the inner life and with the inner and sometimes paradoxical aspects of truth. The Western mind is more literal and practical, inclined to perceive truth more as historic fact and practical good works than as inner development. This does not mean that one approach is right and the other wrong, for wisdom requires us to be both as practical and rational *and* as intuitive and mystic as possible. We are advised by Jung to strengthen the weaker function in ourselves by contact with those who see and feel things differently from ourselves.

But mere contact is not enough; it may even increase resistance to those who differ from us unless we desire to *communicate* with them through what Dr Carl Rogers calls "empathic understanding"; that is, through entering into their minds with imaginative *feeling*, as well as through argument and discussion. If we only do the latter, both sides are beating the air in "psychological space," failing to meet at any point because each is intent on defending his own position. Only when one or other is prepared to drop his defences and to ask, "Tell me exactly how you feel," does real communication, real interthinking and interfeeling become possible; because when A drops his defences and his superiorities, a "miracle" happens and B begins to do the same. In this connection a telling parable appeared in a story called "The Silent Answer" in the Indian magazine *World*.

A space traveler tells of a planet where the highest forms of life were to be best described as "sweet and beautiful and extremely intelligent orangutans." The space traveler racked his brains to find some way of communication with them. Then he remembered the flower sermon of the Buddha. "So I took a flower, beautiful and blue and shaped like a great chalice full of the sweetest nectar, and silently I lifted that as an answer. Immediately I could see by the play of lights in the splendor of the eyes around me, in the soft movements of the diaphanous wings and the caressing touch of the feathery feelers on my arm, that I had been understood. We had discovered that we were more than neighbors; we were one."

Thus can a touch of imagination show that under all the differences that spring only from names, climate and temperament or species, reality is one and the reality of spirit both underpins and transcends all particular lesser loyalties.

From this it can be seen that real tolerance is not the same thing as indifference but that it involves serious education of our thoughts and emotions. There can be no creative thinking without interthinking based on imaginative feeling, and there can be no interthinking without diversity and discussion. If everybody thought alike, no one would think at all. We must therefore, as John Kennedy said, "Make the world safe for diversity."

Totalitarian and authoritarian systems that discourage thought because it may be too disturbing are going against the evolutionary trend of convergence in divergence, of unity in diversity. They are also ignoring that other important truth, that we know only in part and see "as through a glass darkly," like the blind men in the Indian fable groping around an elephant, each misjudging the whole because of his limited contact with the part, and misjudging the part by mistaking it for the whole.

The story is a lesson in the need for humility to admit that we are all very much in the dark and should therefore hold it possible that the light seen by others, whether Greek, Parsee, Sufi, Buddhist or Christian, is essentially the same light of the spirit; that all paths lead ultimately to the same goal, all the colors of the spectrum are needed to demonstrate the richness of white light.

When Jacob Lipschitz, a Lithuanian sculptor, made a symbol of the Virgin for a Catholic church, he wrote on the back: "Jacob Lipschitz, Jew, has made this Virgin for the sake of understanding between men on earth, so that the Spirit may prevail." The next great religious conference to be held should not limit itself to those who believe in Christian doctrine; it should open its doors to all men of good will who believe in and serve "the Holy Ghost, the Lord and Giver of Life"—the spirit which has brought us thus far in the long journey from the dust, which has burned like a steady flame in the great souls of our species, Christian and non-Christian, and which must ultimately come to birth in all men if mankind is to survive.

Where the goal of any religion is increase in the life of the spirit, how do we measure whether one belief structure is superior to another? "Let us frankly recognize," says Radhakrishnan, in *Religion in a Changing World,* "that the efficiency of a religion is to be judged by the development of religious qualities such as quiet confidence, inner calm, gentleness of the spirit, love of neighbor, mercy to all creation, destruction of tyrannous desires, and the aspiration for spiritual freedom. There are no trustworthy statistics to tell us that these qualities are found more in efficient nations." Of all the world's great religions, Matthew Arnold asks:

> Which has not taught weak wills how much they can?
> Which has not fall'n on the dry heart like rain?
> Which has not cried to sunk, self-weary man:
> Thou must be born again!

PART III

Meaning Through Transition

CHAPTER XIV

Tradition and Transition
A Growing Fellowship
for Growing Minds

No tradition is perfect. The best brings only a passing period of peace
or triumph or stable equilibrium; humanity rests for a moment, but
knows that it must travel further; to rest for ever would be to die.
FREYA STARK, *Perseus in the Wind*

The problem is what to do about the dinosaur mentality in our midst.
Survival with freedom today imposes the severest strain on the mechanism of human thinking yet to come before the species. The govern-
ments of the world will not be able to keep this generation from being
incinerated in a nuclear furnace unless they perceive the difference
between tradition and innovation, between habit and insight, between
a mediocre acceptance of existence and a full awareness of the precious-
ness and possibilities of human life.
NORMAN COUSINS, *The Saturday Review,* May 25, 1963

The Church has every reason to see the red light and to be conscious
that it is lagging well behind contemporary ideas of what must be done
to extricate mankind from its perilous situation.
HUGH SCHONFIELD, *Those Incredible Christians*

If the meaning of life is to be found in the sort of growth that
involves inner change and development, where does unchanging
tradition come into the picture? Can these apparent opposites
be reconciled, as in the Hegelian triad, by a third concept that
synthesizes and transcends both? Or must the religious man
choose between being a member of some established religious
sect or dwelling in outer darkness?

The answer of course is no. We can learn to count above two,
and ideally speaking, change and tradition should be working
in harmonious relationship at all times. Otherwise there will be
trouble.

A Japanese was recently quoted as saying, "After thousands of years, everything has suddenly changed; not only external things, but inner attitudes and ways of thinking—everything. Now we concentrate on technical efficiency, but there has to be a balance or we shall lose our bearings."

There has to be a balance as on a tightrope, and there has also to be a sense of direction, a sense that the difficult journey of life leads somewhere. When the Emperor of Japan was believed to be divine, he provided a link between earth and "heaven," between the life we now know and the larger life which the concept of divinity implies. With the loss of such a belief, whether in a divine Emperor or a divine Jehovah, many people abandon all hope of a religious faith that will relate them to life and the cosmos in a meaningful way.

Some decide to settle for material progress in the field of technocracy, and up to a point they are right, for technocracy can rid us of many earthly ills and make life more endurable on the physical plane. But better techniques will not teach us how to live together or how to satisfy our hunger for meaning at a deeper level; neither will being first on the moon give us right of entry into the dimension of spirit that takes away fear of death.

The Japanese was correct in his diagnosis that without a balance we shall lose our bearings. It is a truth that was recognized long ago by the ancient Vedanta. This religious philosophy envisaged the elemental world stuff of mentalized matter as being composed of three forces, or *"gunas," sattva, rajas* and *tamas. Tamas* signified inertia and could be symbolized as a lump of clay; *sattva* was inspiration, or the vision of the artist; and *rajas* was the will-power to overcome inertia and actualize the vision.

The necessity of maintaining this balance applies to all aspects of life, particularly the religious. In organized religion there is a strong tendency to let the tamas of tradition win out over the other two gunas simply because there is a "uroboric" urge in all men to drift back toward that which provides ease and comfort.

> O sweeter than the marriage feast,
> 'Tis sweeter far to me

To walk together to the kirk
With a goodly company.
To walk together to the kirk
And all together pray,
While each to his great Father bends,
Old men and babes and loving friends,
And youths and maidens gay.

There is nothing wrong with this cosy and comforting behavior so long as it is not taken to be the whole of religion; so long as sattva and rajas, inspiration and willed action, are also included.

Erich Neumann, author of *Origins and History of Consciousness,* uses the term "uroboric incest" to describe man's nostalgia for the effortless life of the "womb," the hunger for return to the uroboros, the primordial Great Mother. If the individual does not outgrow this hunger and develop his capacities, he will remain as unconscious or semiconscious as the foetus.

After birth the babe naturally needs the support and comfort of its mother's arms, and the grownup longs to feel that "underneath are the everlasting arms" of the Father God. In plain terms, he longs for the supporting knowledge that life has meaning and that "Someone" — some power or mind or spirit — "means" it.

Tamas has its place both in prenatal and in adult life, but how gladly we welcome signs of growth and interest in the newborn infant. How disturbed we should be to see in him nothing but inertia, to observe nothing but escapist fantasy as he grows older. Yet all too often institutional religion, especially in its authoritarian forms, makes no expectation of further growth, regards passive obedience as a priority, and frowns on independent thinking. "The Captain has spoken. When your Captain gives orders, you don't argue, you obey," was the comment of one priest on the Pope's Birth Control Encyclical.

The lethargic mind that likes to be told what to do and what to think will accept the voice of authority as unquestioningly as Casabianca on the burning deck. For the thoughtful, there are other possibilities.

Someone has said, "The great debate of our time rages between . . . the traditionalists and the existentialists. The

former insist on keeping the inherited house tidy; the latter
on discarding it and building it anew." The statement is an
oversimplification, for few people are quite so extremist. The
former are generally willing to allow a little of the "untidi-
ness" caused by freedom of thought, and the latter to admit the
value of retaining some traditions. Both have their place in
life, and the problem is not which of them is right but when,
and how much, and under what circumstances it is wise to stress
the one or the other.

Somewhere between the extremes lies wisdom, and wisdom
recognizes that life must be always moving forward and also
that whatever is valid in the past must be retained. To be
completely cut off from our religious roots, without any germ
of new life and thought growing within us to replace them, is
to be in the pitiable condition of Estragon and Vladimir forever "waiting for Godot"; waiting, that is, for someone to come
along and tell us the meaning of life, someone to cure the sense
of emptiness and of the void. That "there's no lack of void,"
as Vladimir put it, is being constantly demonstrated today in
the statements that come from thoughtful and articulate youth.
The following letter from an American boy illustrates the
necessity of a growing religion:

> I am a sixteen-year-old senior in a square high school. I have a
> good home and kind parents who tell me that I should work hard
> in school in order to go to a good college so that I can get a good
> job and make more money.
> This does not seem to me the real purpose of life. It does not
> seem to be what I want. But I don't know what it is that I do
> want. Maybe it's sex, but I don't think so. I keep looking. I seem
> to need to know what I am and what God is, but I can't find any
> help in my church. I feel a love for all people, but until I can
> find myself I am helpless. Can you help me?

Not only the young but people of all ages feel lost when something causes them to question the static theology on which they
have been nurtured. An eighty-year-old Englishwoman once
knocked on her vicar's door and made the "shocking" admission,
"Vicar, I've lost my faith." Having been immutably conditioned
to think of religion in terms of believing Christian doctrine
rather than in terms of inner growth in which honest doubt

has its place, all the vicar could think of was to promise to pray for her return to the fold.

Many modern church leaders are ready and wanting to change some of the language and concepts of traditional Christianity, but the problem is what to keep, what to reject, or what to regard as symbolic. Some say there should be no compromise with the central story of God's intervention in Jesus Christ, that this particular concept must stand "firm as a rock." But how can it, when so many deeply religious people do not and cannot believe it? They believe not that God intervened by sending his only son into the world to save us, but that it was Jesus who did the invading of another dimension of being, the unobstructed universe of spirit.

This is surely a more reasonable hypothesis and one that brings a greater hope to man. Instead of being offered salvation through that cruel death, we are given the sattva, the inspiration of his life and the promise: "The works that I do shall ye do also." Sattva is needed in order to get rajas working on tamas. We need inspiration to rouse us out of our lethargy, and modern man can find such inspiration in the knowledge that further mutation is possible, mutation that can open up to him the reality of higher worlds, as it did for Jesus and all Mahatmas. We can know more only as we become more and are consequently able to see more. This is the concept that synthesizes the apparent opposites of tradition and change. We have to keep firm as a rock the eternal verities of love, courage and beauty, and we also have to change and grow and fulfil our highest potentiality, as the Parable of the Sower teaches.

To "protest too much," week by week, that Jesus is God is to create tedium in the minds of the hearers. It would be more effective to take the words spoken to Nicodemus more seriously and relate them to the modern teaching of psychosynthesis and evolution concerning the responsibility for realizing our full potentialities.

"We are at the end of an era, with the old theological systems a shambles," says Dr James McCord, president of Princeton Theological Seminary.

In that case we should not go on bolstering up the systems

but should meet the present challenge by trying to understand religion in depth, the way Jesus understood it, and by shifting the emphasis in the direction that Archbishop Frederick Temple urged over a hundred years ago. He then wrote: "Our theology has been cast in a scholastic mold; that is, all based on logic. We are in need of, and we are gradually being forced into, a theology based on psychology. The transition, I fear, will not be without much pain; but nothing can prevent it."

The long delay in the making of this transition cannot be placed entirely at the door of the clergy. Academic psychology has had little to offer them, and psychoanalysis has seemed to many to be a rather distasteful delving into those aspects of the unconscious psyche which are "best forgotten." Moreover, the Freudian approach has appeared to be positively inimical to religion.

This apparent enmity was largely due to Freud's book *The Future of An Illusion,* in which he mistakenly identified religion with doctrines that he regarded, rightly or wrongly, as the expression of unconscious wishes and desires. In his later life he developed a deeper understanding of religion as such.

Today, however, there are two branches of psychological study that should be of the greatest possible help to the churches and their teachers. There is the school now known as psycho-synthesis or logotherapy. In an address given at an international congress of psychotherapy, Dr Robert Assagioli said of it, "The value of the existential approach is that it goes deep down to the core of the patient's trouble, which is connected with his whole personality. It takes into account his attitude to life and aims at correcting and changing it in a constructive way."

As Dr Viktor Frankl puts it, "Every therapy must in some way also be logotherapy." That is to say, it must give the patient philosophic meaning as well as psychological understanding. It must recognize the spiritual aspect of man as well as the instinctual.

Secondly there is the straightforward educational and child psychology as taught to all young teachers in training. This has at last begun to find its way into official religious teaching, and religious instruction is now in the process of becoming religious education. Soon it will dawn on all who deal with children that to bore them is the best way of alienating them from the subject.

"I never took in a word of it," said a man who had once been a cathedral chorister. "I liked the singing, but the lessons and prayers flowed over me as so much meaningless verbiage and developed in me a habit of inattention."

"Jesus bores me," was the startling confession of an older youth.

Pandering to children is as undesirable as undue severity, and a certain amount of boredom is inevitable in life and must be endured. But those with even the most elementary knowledge of educational psychology know that if a lesson is to have life and to stimulate effort it must relate to the interests and understanding of the child mind. Otherwise it will lack the sattva of inspiration.

As Joyce Cary writes: "We had our Bible lessons, of course, but the religion which actually stayed with us was something braver, keener than the church teaching. A lecture from a boy's parent, a sailor, about chasing dhows in the Gulf, went to the bottom of our feelings in one flash."

By contrast, one confused teacher, concerned about the lack of religious instruction in her school, announced: "I was determined that they should hear the name of God at least once a week."

It does not matter whether God is mentioned by name so long as the heart is tuned to the finer issues. Only very occasionally does the reading of the Old Testament do this. For the most part, the minister's words "Here endeth the Lesson" are inwardly greeted with a sigh of thankfulness. Would it be too revolutionary for the audience to be given some idea of the significance of the so-called "Lesson" beforehand? Or to let them have a change by hearing a reading from some other inspirational literature than that of the ancient Hebrews?

Children to whom the Bible has been presented as a sort of sacred mascot, containing all truth, are becoming very confused by the difference between its teaching and the teaching of science on such matters as evolution. "This is my Bible," said one young student, referring to Loren Eiseley's inspiring book *The Immense Journey.*

When consulted by Professor Jowett of Oxford about the compilation of a Children's Bible, Florence Nightingale sent with her list of suitable stories this comment: "There are some things in Homer we might better call 'Holy Writ,' many, many in Sophocles and Aeschylus. The stories about Andromache and Antigone are worth all the women in the Old Testament put together. The story of Achilles and his horse is far more fit for children than that of Balaam and his ass."

The theologian Paul Tillich suggested that no final theology should ever be claimed, and that each generation should evolve its own interpretations, building on the past.

This is the most fundamental type of religious education. It can take place only in relation to actual situations and among people who trust and respect one another. Ruth Robinson, whose husband wrote *The New Reformation,* was concerned that her children should not be deprived of whatever was valuable in their Christian heritage, but that at the same time they should think things out for themselves as they went along and should build up religious attitudes in relation to the problems that arose in the course of daily living. In this way there would be no need for later unlearning or loss of faith, for they would believe only what they themselves had personally explored and found to be true in experience. In discussing life's problems with them, the mother followed the lead of her children, only relating their joint finding to bible or church teaching where these might be relevant.

This is an educationally sound approach, for religion is a matter of growth in the course of which the understanding of spiritual values slowly unfolds; it is not a matter of believing what authority teaches, of short-cut conversions, or of experiences artificially induced through hallucinogens.

Dante described how, in his long pilgrimage, "By slow degrees, new truth would meet my view," a hard saying for those who want clear and definite answers and want them *now.* We must outgrow such childish demands and learn to travel with some uncertainty and some insecurity. For as a verse by Balfour says:

Our highest truths are but half-truths.
Think not to settle down for ever in any truth;
Make use of it as a tent in which to spend a summer's night
But build no house on it, or it will be your tomb.
When first you have an inkling of its insufficiency
And begin to decry a dim countertruth looming up beyond,
It is the Lord's voice whispering
"Take up thy bed and walk."

Training his students to live with some ignorance and some
uncertainties, Albert Schweitzer gave them the following warning: "When you preach the Gospel, beware of preaching it as
the religion that explains everything." For ten years before he
went to Africa he was preparing boys in Strasburg for Confirmation. In *Christianity and the Religions of the World* he writes that
"After the war, some of them came to see me and thanked me
for having taught them so definitely that religion was not a
formula for explaining everything. They said it had been that
teaching which had kept them from discarding Christianity,
whereas so many others in the trenches discarded it, not being
prepared to meet the inexplicable."

Indeed the "Christian" Schweitzer went far to bridge the gulf
between believer and disbeliever in his teaching that only in proportion as we have the Spirit of Jesus do we have true knowledge
of Jesus; historical knowledge about him is of no importance.
"The abiding and eternal in Jesus is absolutely independent
of historical knowledge and can only be understood by contact
with his spirit, which is still at work in the world." *(Quest of the
Historical Jesus.)*

But "spirit" as already said, is a difficult word to define or
understand, especially for those not accustomed to thinking in
abstract or universal terms. "It" has therefore been symbolized
in various ways; as a dove descending out of heaven, or as flames
of fire, or as the third "Person" of the Trinity. Today we try to
imagine it as an invisible power or presence, the life force, the
new dimension of being that awaits our attainment. It is the
basic element of all traditional religions, before the time of Jesus,
Socrates or the Buddha. It is inherent in the great evolutionary
process and it is what makes possible the evolution of the indi-

vidual; for as Vedanta puts it, *Tat Tvam Asi*, "Thou art that," or, "The spirit is in you."

Early in the Christian era the insight of Abelard saw that "the reign of the Father and of the Son is ended; the reign of the Spirit is begun" — for which statement he was, not surprisingly, persecuted. For the most part we are not yet mature enough to grasp his meaning, but we have the word of a modern theologian, Nicholas Berdyaev, that "the religion of the Spirit will be the religion of man when he comes of age." *(Destiny of Man.)*

The journey to spiritual maturity is long delayed, and meanwhile we continue to overemphasize the secondary aspects of religious tradition and waste time disputing over these, so that even "Christians" cannot manage to unite "in the unity of the spirit which is the bond of peace." Still less can they imagine uniting with men of other traditions in that spirit. "Christ the hope of the world," the clarion cry of the World Council of Churches, is meaningless unless it refers to the Christ-spirit, which is the same as the spirit of Jesus, of Milarepa, Gautama, Akhnaton and all dedicated seekers after the things of the spirit; of truth, goodness, love and beauty.

Nothing that has been said here is intended to suggest that people should give up the church of their particular tradition so long as that tradition has meaning for them and helps them to keep their lives in order. Moreover, there are times when, even for the agnostic, nothing else has yet been devised to meet his very real emotional need. After attending the funeral of Maynard Keynes, the free thinker, Kingsley Martin somewhat surprisingly wrote in *The New Statesman:*

> I suppose only a minute percentage of those at the Keynes Memorial Service in Westminster Abbey actually accepted in any simple sense the doctrines and beliefs embodied in the words of the hymns and prayers in which they joined. Certainly Keynes, a staunch rationalist, would not have done so.
> And yet none of us would have been willing to forego the service, or felt inclined to criticize the words. They were singularly well chosen; they were all familiar. And it was because they were familiar that they meant so much, so much more than their superificial content.
> Rationalism has argued the Church out of existence, yet not dethroned it; mainly I think because although men no longer be-

lieve in the Judaic God whom they evoke they do demand on the great occasions of life—birth, marriage, death and festival—a ceremony to satisfy their emotions, and to celebrate the occasion in community.

Tradition cannot be invented, nor can consciously devised ceremonial take the place of words whose associations are so much more important than their surface meanings.

A London Diary

Yet Kingsley Martin asked that there should be no religious service at his funeral in 1969.

Another "agnostic," Nehru, preserved an "unnecessary" bit of traditional symbolism when he asked in his will that a handful of his ashes be cast into the Ganges at Allahabad. He explained that the Ganges had been to him a symbol and a memory of the past of India running into the present and flowing into the future. He said, "I had discarded much of past tradition and custom and am anxious that India should rid herself of all shackles that bind and constrain her and divide her people and prevent free development of the body and the spirit. But though I seek all this, yet I do not wish to cut myself off from that past completely. I am proud of that great inheritance that has been and is ours; and I am conscious that I too am a link in that unbroken chain that goes back to the dawn of history."

There are, then, two possible pitfalls that confront the seeker. He can sever all connection with the past and be left with a vacuum; or he can cling tenaciously to the past, fearing that any change in it might bring the whole belief-system toppling. The vital and growing mind learns to find its way between these pitfalls, to retain what still seems valid in the past and at the same time to rid itself of "disreputable shackles." Many find their solution by going into church only when it is empty or when music is being played. Meditation can be of more value than petitionary prayer.

The struggle to find a balance between rigidity and change is endless and is soluble only in terms of tolerance and a deepening of understanding, not by trying to prove who is right. The erstwhile Jesuit priest Charles Davis felt obliged to leave his church because he found it cared more for tradition than for truth or for people.

The Papal Court of Rome has made some important advances of late, especially in denouncing the Holy Office as a "stumbling-block and a scandal." But in its continuing refusal to allow priests to marry or women to plan their own families by medically approved means, it shows an incomprehensible rigidity. Quite apart from the grave dangers of the population explosion, it is obvious that an overprolific and worn out mother of twelve cannot draw out the highest quality either in herself or her children.

Inflexibility tends to boomerang in unforeseen ways. By refusing to let the paleontologist Teilhard de Chardin lecture in the Sorbonne, the Roman Church opened the way for him to go to China, where he made important new discoveries, now presented to the world in books that have enabled theologians to view their ideas in the new perspective of evolution and perhaps also opened the eyes of some scientists to the spiritual implication of their knowledge.

For it is not only theologians who need to stretch their minds toward further horizons. There are some scientists who limit the quest for knowledge to their own particular area of interest, where everything is based on reason and tested by reason, and they are as contemptuous of any other order of knowledge, such as mystic experience or extrasensory perception, as the narrow fundamentalist is contemptuous of the scientist. Both miss out on the goal of wholeness. *Spiritual experience is* a reality, and therefore it is unscientific to ignore it.

The scientific method is a valid approach to new knowledge but not the only approach, and scientific facts are not the only kind of knowledge. In every form of research, willingness to entertain a hypothesis is not only admissible but vital to any advance.

"The ever-new life should ever create the school anew," said the educational philosopher Herbart. His words apply not only to school, but also to church, state, or any other institution. If the tradition handed down is not open to new thoughts and new insights, the blood begins to harden in the brain cells and we find ourselves mechanically repeating the words and attitudes that custom dictates, instead of living flexibly and creatively as life requires. This happens when we think of truth as something static and final, which is contained in a book or a body of doctrines or a person, rather than as something that slowly emerges as we work our way toward it.

The problem, as Norman Cousins says, is "what to do about the dinosaur mentality in our midst" and the inertia in ourselves. Man, with his terrifying weapons of war, should not risk remaining for ever "a child of Cain" or life will throw him aside. The need now is not for greater numbers of people but for a higher quality of consciousness; it is, in Loren Eiseley's words, for "a gentler, a more tolerant people than those who won for us against the ice, the tiger and the bear." It is for people capable of thinking and feeling *in depth* as well as in surface extensity.

Thinking in depth removes the need to cling to any specific tradition and reveals that all the varied expressions of religious faith may contribute something to the truth about the nature of reality. Speaking of the fifteenth-century poet Kabir, Evelyn Underhill says that "he seems by turns Vedantist and Vaishnavite, Brahman and Sufi, Pantheist and Transcendentalist," and, "In thus adapting traditional materials to his own use, he follows a method common among the mystics, who . . . will pour their wine into almost any vessel that comes to hand; generally using by preference—and lifting to new levels of significance—the religious or philosophic formulae current in their own day."

Traditional Christianity went off the rails in teaching that "salvation" depends on "correct" belief. Fortunately the word is in process of acquiring a new meaning—or rather of recovering its truer meaning. For the salvation man now feels he needs is not salvation from a hell of eternal punishment in the hereafter, but salvation from the hell he is creating on earth through his failure to achieve a higher level of consciousness.

Psychoanalyst James Hillman writes, in *Suicide and Soul,* "We find that behind all urges to grow and develop, to create and produce, to hope for more strength and more life and more time, behind the 'go, go, go', is the need to save one's soul one way or another, by hook or by crook, through hell and high water, by Zen, or by Freud or by Jung. Through the direct experience made possible in analysis, we do as the Buddha said: work at our own salvation with diligence." Not only the Buddha but the ancient Vedas taught the same:

No one saves us but ourselves,
No one can and no one may.
Others only point the path,
We ourselves must walk the Way.

CHAPTER XV

The Great Transition

The Scientific Approach

We must follow up all the clues of untapped possibilities like extrasensory perception. They may prove to be as important and extraordinary as the once unsuspected electrical possibilities of matter.

JULIAN HUXLEY

"And does everyone die?" asked a little boy anxiously.

"Yes," replied his mother, "that is the way of it. We all have
to die."

To some young children, the word "death" is phonetically
terrifying and they hate to hear it spoken. "I wouldn't mind so
much if they called it 'hig,'" was the comment of another small
child.

The word does have a final sound, but it has yet to be proved
that death is a final event. Perhaps if it could be shown that it is
merely a transition, the word itself would cease to alarm us.
Bertrand Russell once wrote, "I would scorn to be afraid to die,"
but it may be that there is a deep-rooted unconscious fear of
annihilation, barely recognized, in all men, and the fear may be
less for ourselves than for our loved ones. "Though he slay me,"
said Job, "yet will I trust," but what if he slay my beloved? Then
we hear that exceeding bitter cry· "Would God I had died for
thee, O Absalom my son, my son."

It is not surprising that some mourners in their grief turn to
spiritualism for reassurance. Unfortunately, whatever sign
might be found in this sphere is rendered suspect on one hand
by exploitation of grief through fraudulent practices and on

the other hand by too-eager readiness to believe, causing self delusion.

This, however, should not mean closing the door on all careful scientific study of the subject. Under the title of psychic research, or parapsychology, the study of extrasensory perception, which includes spiritualism, is now being taken seriously. If the findings of this research do not as yet provide clear proof of post-mortal existence, they have at least provided sufficient evidence to justify keeping the door open on such a possibility. The self-styled realist or logical positivist who is sure that nothing unprovable by logic can be true should think again, or he may one day get the surprise of his life.

The old-fashioned materialist, for whom the definition of matter was "that which has weight and can be measured," argued that since we have no experience of mind existing independently of matter, the probability that it can do so is negligible. But now that man has fissioned and fused the atom (hitherto regarded as a small particle of solid matter) and has revealed the mighty potential force contained therein, we no longer know precisely what matter is. We are told that the very chair on which we sit is composed of myriads of electrons, protons, neutrons, and other particles, all whirling round at a prodigious speed. What the scientists tell us must be true so far as it goes, although in everyday living we act as if it were not, because we do not know of any other way to act.

Professor Margenau says, "Some ideas of current physics are as difficult to grasp as are those of parapsychology," and this idea that matter is a form of potential force is surely one such idea. He adds, "It is necessary to invoke the existence of 'virtual processes' which follow no ordinary law. . . . In a very short time, every physical process can proceed in ways which defy the laws of nature known today, always hiding itself under the principle of uncertainty to be sure."

That *uncertainty* should be regarded as a principle is difficult for the dogmatist in all of us to accept. We like things to be definite, clearcut, true or false, right or wrong. "I like him because he's sure of himself; he knows what he thinks and speaks out clearly. You know where you are with him," said one young voter of her favorite candidate. But maturity requires that we be uncertain about many things and be willing to look deeply into the complexities of life, even at the risk of finding what we fear to see.

We all know the story of the medieval monk who refused to look through Galileo's telescope in case he should see the moons round Jupiter in whose existence he could not believe because Aristotle, his scientific authority, had never mentioned them. We smile with superiority at such pitiful narrowness, but there are some not immune from prejudice among scientists themselves — men who cannot tolerate the thought of their own particular "orthodoxy's" being disturbed· by "virtual processes," or of hypotheses that "defy the laws of nature known today," as does extrasensory perception.

However, there are master minds of greater depth and breadth — and "insight men" like William James, Henry Sidgwick, Gilbert Murray, Sigmund Freud, and Cyril Burt, to mention only a few — who have known that there is too much scientifically based evidence of ESP to justify its being ignored or regarded as unworthy of serious study. Parapsychology cannot prove survival after death, any more than logic can prove or disprove the existence of God, but if its claim to have proved telepathy is valid, this means that thought and feeling can exist independently of "matter" — which is much the same as mind's existing independently of body.

It is not possible for Christians to be sure what is legendary and what is historical in the Gospel story, but if there really were people who believed they had seen Jesus alive after the crucifixion there is nothing unusual about that. Numerous are the cases of intelligent and sincere individuals who have, without expecting it, had similar surprising experiences. It is certain that people sometimes see the spirits of, or receive messages from, the "dead," but the nature of the form that appears to them is beyond our ken.

In *The Theory of Eternal Life,* Rodney Collin conceives of "a chain-movement upwards into *higher matter.* . . . There are inherent in the universe many degrees of immortality. Each world of matter is immortal in relation to the denser world below. The molecular world is immortal in relation to the cellular world of nature, which periodically dies and is reborn upon its surface. The electronic or solar world of light is immortal in relation to the molecular world of earth. And a being possessing a body of the nature and matter of one such world must enjoy potential immortality in relation to beings inhabiting the world below."

What Collin is saying is that grades of "material" and physical development show a correlation with grades of mental and spiritual development, and that the sort of immortality we may achieve will correspond to the grade of spiritual being that we have reached. "Thus if a man having full control over a cellular body is immortal and omnipotent in the world of mineral bodies, a man having full control over a molecular body or soul may in turn be immortal and omnipotent in the world of cellular bodies. And a man having full control over an electronic body or spirit will be immortal and omnipotent in the world of molecular bodies ... that is, in the world of men's souls." He goes on to imply that Jesus could have been such a one, having himself a "body" of divine or spiritual energy that gave him power to fashion the souls of men — or, better, to help them fashion their own souls.

This, however, does not mean independently of any kind of "material" structure, such as invisible electric waves. Obviously there must be many more invisible things in the universe than we have yet discovered, for as we now are, it is as if our eyes were only sensitive to one octave of light rays, or our hearing to one octave of sound.

We are only at the beginning of knowledge, and our imaginations are very limited. But experience should remind us that there is often a third alternative to what at first presents itself as a simple opposition, an "either-or," and the third alternative here would be not mind or body as we know them but a new kind of structure, something that we slowly build up during our lifetime. St Paul called it "a spiritual body," which from the human and rational standpoint is a contradiction in terms. The alchemists spoke of the quintessential, subtle, or diamond body. Others have spoken of astral, etheric or psychic bodies — at any rate, "something" that is related to, yet different from, both body and mind as they appear to our present powers of perception. It is not possible to imagine what this may be like, but

Harold Goddard gives us a useful analogy in *The Meaning of Shakespeare*: "Imagination," he says, "is . . . as if the birds, unable to understand the speech of man, and man unable to understand the songs of birds, yet longing to communicate, were to agree on a tongue made up of sounds they both could comprehend, the voice of running water perhaps, or the wind in the trees."

As logic teaches, a proposition can have only one opposite but many possible alternatives. If we could envisage a satisfactory alternative structure, this would be a case of what Jung calls the "reconciling image." This, while departing from the province of pure science (if there is such a thing), is an interesting hypothesis; and it is justifiable to entertain hypotheses that can lead to fresh levels of understanding, so long as they are not given the status of verified fact until they have been checked by a disciplined reason. Reason, intuition, insight and imagination all have their place in the pursuit of truth, and no one of them must try to take over full command from the others. In any case, since life and death are part of one process, it follows that the more we can discover about the meaning and the laws of life, the more we shall be able to understand about the significance of death. And if the trend of the great evolutionary process is in fact toward ever higher levels of consciousness, it is not unreasonable to hypothesize that, in a growing personality, that process continues after the bodily shell has been outgrown, even though we cannot imagine how.

The fact that we cannot imagine the mode of its existence is no argument, for we could never have imagined many of the things that science now pronounces to be factually true, for example the presence and power of electricity in the universe and man's ability to harness and control it. Seventy-odd years ago it sounded like a miracle when we were told that soon we should no longer need oil lamps but could have something called electric light by the turning of a switch. Equally strange is it to hear that the colors of the rainbow, which look "real" enough, are not there when we turn our back on them; that the scent of the rose and the green of the grass depend on a mind in order to be known. Professor Whitehead rather surprisingly says, "Nature is a dull affair, soundless, senseless, colorless, merely the hurrying of material, endlessly, meaninglessly. It is qualities of the human mind that clothe and color it."

This is all very strange, but the truth is that the more science tells us about this surprising world, the more "miraculous" it becomes. Those who feel quite sure that the very idea of an afterlife is preposterous should consider the words of Macneile Dixon, author of *The Human Situation*:

> For myself, I have no affection for fixed ideas. My mistrust of them and of all that seems certain and obvious is profound. Had I been present at the birth of this planet I would probably not have believed on the word of an archangel that the blazing mass, the incandescent whirlpool there before our eyes at a temperature of 50 million degrees, would presently set about the establishment of empires and civilizations, that it was on its way to produce Greek art and Italian painting, would tolerate such things as music and mathematics, make room for optimists and pessimists, admit the arrival of Homers, Beethovens and Napoleons. I would have listened most respectfully to the archangel who predicted these singular occurrences, but I would have whispered to myself, "He is a romantic." So it is that I have become a confirmed skeptic in respect of precipitate and headlong conclusions.

It is therefore unwise to dismiss anything as preposterous simply because it seems incredible. Even modern scientific man can be fooled by his incredulity. When Edison's phonograph was first shown to the Paris Academy of Sciences, the scientists present insisted that it was impossible to reproduce the human voice by means of a metal disc; there must be a ventriloquist concealed somewhere! Scientists are supposed to be detached, neither credulous nor incredulous, but in fact they are often, like the ordinary man, governed by their emotions.

Professor Broad, Knightbridge Professor of Moral Philosophy at Cambridge, says that he "would be slightly more annoyed than surprised" if he found himself in some sense persisting after the immediate death of his body. He cannot therefore be accused of prejudice in favor of survival when he admits the possibility of a nonphysical "something" in which man's self could function after death. He writes, "If survival be conceivable, then I cannot but think that the least implausible form of the hypothesis would be that, at any rate immediately after death and for some indefinite period later, the surviving personality is embodied in some kind of nonphysical body, which was during life associated in some way with the physical body. If so, I should think it quite likely that many surviving personalities would—as Swedenborg alleges that they do—at first and for some considerable time afterwards, confuse this nonphysical body with their former physical one and fail to realize that they have died."

One of the most interesting explorations yet made into the realm of the paranormal is that described in the books of Stewart Edward White in which he writes of working with his wife in this sphere both before and after her death. In *The Unobstructed Universe* she speaks to him through what she calls her "station," Joan: "The limitations of human existence vary according to the individual. The mode of existence of certain individuals is farther out into the whole. Grant that, and you immediately grant that you have a shifting line, an unfixed horizon, even in your own universe.... How different do you suppose that your existing universe is to you than it is to a child?"

That is indeed a fascinating thought. Dr. Ward tells us that to the newborn babe, the world around him is "a big blooming, buzzing confusion," yet it is the same world perceived by the grown man as a place of endless interest, wonder and beauty. But the grown man foolishly supposes that he is seeing all that there is. It is not only our "estrangéd faces" but our still immature stage of development that causes us to "miss the many-splendored thing." The difference of comprehension between two "grown-up" men is often as great or greater than that between a child and a man. The tripper accosts the poet, lost in ecstasy over the beauty of the Lake District, with the petulant question, "Is there anything to see in this place?"

The explanation of *The Unobstructed Universe* continues: "There is no division. The only difference really between our worlds is a difference of frequency. If you can discover the frequency, you can reveal my universe.... The only reason you cannot exist and operate in the *entire* universe—as I do—for I operate in your universe as well as mine—is because you are not able to step up your frequency."

This was illustrated by reference to the electric fan, whose frequency is so rapid that it appears to lose solidity and to become unobstructed or permeable to sight. Mr White is told, "If the frequency were different for your human focus, you could see me. As it is, you look through me. I am not there. . . . I live in the *whole* universe, the one you see and also the one you do not see. I operate in your universe as well as mine but for me yours is unobstructed; for you it is obstructed."

The natural human tendency is to suppose that only the familiar can be true, and if any new thought is a challenge to our own vested intellectual and emotional interests we often have been ready to annihilate those who expressed it. Giordano Bruno was cruelly tormented and burned for revealing his discovery that the earth turns on its axis round the sun. Slowly the world grows more tolerant and flexible and can accept, or at least show interest in, the findings of the new science of ESP, or parapsychology, no matter how unfamiliar and surprising they may seem.

Professor H. H. Price, formerly Wykeham Professor of Logic at Oxford, says, "Telepathy is something which ought not to happen at all if the materialistic theory were true. But it does happen. So there must be something seriously wrong with the materialistic theory, however numerous and imposing the normal facts which support it may be."

So while science, or the scientific method, has not yet completely proved the existence of life after death, neither has it proved the opposite. It is in fact not possible to prove a negative, and to some highly intelligent people the possibility of an afterlife seems no more remarkable than many other "miracles" surrounding us that we take for granted. Therefore the scientist must at least keep an open mind while following up all clues to the existence of untapped possibilities. To dismiss these from motives of dislike or prejudice is definitely unscientific. The physicist tells us that a "solid" stone is in fact a "whirlpool of furious motions." Fantastic as the information sounds, today we meekly believe him instead of putting him to death, because the authority of science has largely replaced the authority of the church.

CHAPTER XVI

The Great Transition
The Inner Significance of Death

> I died from the plant and reappeared in an animal;
> I died from the animal and became a man;
> Wherefore then should I fear?
> When did I grow less by dying?
>
> Next time I shall die from the man,
> That I may grow the wings of angels
> From the angel too must I advance;
> "ALL THINGS SHALL PERISH SAVE HIS FACE."
> *Koran XXV,* ii, 88.

> Once more shall I wing my way above the angels;
> I shall become that which entereth not the imagination.
> Then let me become naught, naught; for the harp string crieth unto me
> "Verily unto Him do we return."
> JALALU'D-DIN RUMI (Persian poet)

Many people are quite sure that death ends all and has no other significance. Some are even glad that it should be so, in case a future life should be anything like a continuation of this one. They prefer to think they will "go out like a candle" and have the consolation of knowing that "If I am not, I care not."

Some of these are admirable people, modern humanists who find sufficient satisfaction in the pursuit of knowledge and the service of their fellow men. Others, like those of the Old Testament times, have a profound faith in God and the immense importance of righteous living but none in an afterlife, (*Psalm CXV,* 17: "The dead praise not the Lord, neither any that go down into the silence"); or they believe that if there is such a thing, it is, as with the ancient Greeks, in a dreary underworld.

(*Ecclesiastes IX, 10.* ". . . for there is no work, nor device, nor knowledge, nor wisdom in the grave whither thou goest.") There were a few exceptions, like the patriarch Job, who although at one time he assumed "Man is cut down like a flower and continueth not" (*Job XIV, 1*), yet when his trials were over, uttered those triumphant words that still are in the Christian burial service nearly 2000 years later (*Job XIX, 25/6*)*:* "I know that my redeemer liveth, and that he shall stand at the latter day upon the earth."

So we should not be ruled by our ignorance or allow our limited imaginations to make dogmatic negative statements, for we cannot prove a negative. The truth is that we can find significance in death only if we have found it in life.

Let us begin by admitting that everything in life is in a state of impermanence and that death is an inherent and inevitable part of the life process; that living and dying are not separable; and that, as stated in the brief Gospel parable: "Except a grain of wheat fall into the ground and die, it abideth alone: but if it die, it bringeth forth much fruit." (*John XII, 24. N.E.B.*)

However, the relation between living and dying, so obvious in plant life, is not so obvious in the human sphere. A young Buddhist, coming to this country for the first time, commented, "I have noticed that you rejoice over the birth of a child and weep over a death. Please, why?" His religion had taught him to see man's time on this planet as a period of training, a stage in process of growth toward a higher condition of being. Why, therefore, weep over death, which should, when the new "spirit-body" has been adequately developed, be a glad entry into a higher state of consciousness in which we shall be able to grow and learn indefinitely, *in this same universe* but with new powers and in new "vehicles," freed from the "obstructions" caused by the dense "matter" in which we now have to function.

Fear of Death
Francis Bacon's famous essay tells us that "Men fear death as children fear to go into the dark." Certainly fear of death, for ourselves as well as for our loved ones, does appear to be innate, even if Freud is right that we also have a death-wish. Christians

are given the assurance that "As in Adam all die, even so in Christ shall all be made alive." The "Resurrection" of Jesus is taken as guaranteeing this, provided we believe it. To believe it is to be "saved." In fact, Paul went so far as to say, "If Christ be not risen, then is our preaching vain, and your faith is also vain. Ye are yet in your sins." (*I Corinthians, XV*, 14.) The last six words show that the Easter story signified to Paul not merely the promise of eternal life, but what evidently concerned him just as much, the atoning quality of the crucifixion. "He was delivered to death for our misdeeds, and raised to life to justify us" (*Romans IV*, 25, *N.E.B.*). Paul's overpowering sense of guilt has bedeviled Christian teaching with its doctrine of atonement for 1900 years, but it is not that kind of "salvation" with which we are here concerned.

The Greeks, like the Buddhists, seem to have thought more about the excellence of man than his sinfulness. At any rate, what the mystery religions, popular in Greece and round the Mediterranean in Paul's day, were trying at their best to effect through a ritual symbolic "death" was freedom from fear of actual bodily death, and also the realization that it is possible to transcend the human condition as we know it and, through "death," to obtain a higher mode of being.

This is what Jesus tried to explain to Nicodemus, but the latter understood nothing of the language of regeneration and rebirth, because these concepts were Greek, not Jewish.

We know all too little of the detailed nature of the mystery ceremonies, but we do know that those at Eleusis, outside Athens, were highly thought of even by Aristotle, who himself finally reached the conclusion that "Death is no evil; death is a good," and by Plato, who said, "To die is to be initiated."

Unlike the ceremonies of primitive tribes that were intended to initiate youth into manhood, the purpose of the mysteries was religious in that they sought, through ritual death followed by experience of new life, to give the initiate conquest over fear of death of the body and belief in the possibility of spiritual survival for those who had developed spiritual being during this life.

Naturally, not all of those who took part in the ceremony received its message. It was said at the time, "Many bear the palm but few are the mystes"—the ones who could understand its significance. Then as now, the majority found it easier to worship the god with whom the ceremony was sometimes associated than to grasp the meaning of the teaching, *Mors janua vitae*: Death is the gate of life.

The old story of salvation through the sacrificial death of a savior, mythical or historical, has become meaningless to modern man, who would regard a god requiring anything so terrible as being himself in need of salvation. Yet there is a sense in which we need to be "saved," not so much from our "sins" of commission as from failure to find our true selves, to "miss the mark of the high calling"; failure to become what we potentially are and to discover for ourselves the truth that "Death has no dominion over us" because

Birthless and deathless and changeless remaineth the spirit forever;
Death cannot touch it at all, dead though the house of it seems.

The Bhagavad-Gîta

The Art of Creative Living
Since we have no special ceremonies like those of the Greek mystery religions, whose purpose was to induce in the initiate a sense of the creative relationship between life and death and so to perceive both as meaningful, where today can the young turn to find spiritual meaning for what Mircea Eliade calls this "desacrilized existence"? At the moment they are turning in large numbers to the arts, and this is good in that all aspects of beauty, whether in color, form, movement, or sound, can give openings on to the beyond and so become pathways for the ascent of consciousness. But it is not enough. Frustration, misery and suicide are not unknown among art students. They, like other people, have to face suffering sooner or later.

The art of living includes and transcends the lesser arts, but it has received all too little attention from churches, schools or colleges. A breakthrough has, however, recently been made in the sphere of psychotherapy offering a great hope for man's better understanding of, and power over, himself. What is now called logotherapy or psychosynthesis is not so much concerned with finding the deep-seated causes of man's ills in the early frustrations of his instinctive life, as it is with showing him that he has within him the germ of potential new life, a seed of the spirit. Once a man discovers this, he need no longer dwell in an "existential vacuum," for he has found the source of meaning that will carry him forward through death. It is hard for those who have been taught to regard themselves only as "miserable sinners," in need of an external savior, to believe the "startling" words of the poet James Rhoades:

> Know this, O man; sole root of sin in thee
> Is not to know thine own divinity.

It is immensely inspiring that a brave, tormented psychologist should have had the interest to test the truth of those words amid the horrors of the concentration camps and should also have had the courage to publish his findings in the critical academic world. Viktor Frankl, an Austrian psychiatrist who lost all his family save one in concentration camps and spent four years in them himself, found that the response to spiritual values could, in a few men and women, still persist, or even awaken for the first time, when all surrounding circumstances conspired to make the sufferers lose their hold.

This aspect of the psyche is something psychologists have hitherto ignored in their textbooks and their lectures. Its re-discovery should go far to establish the connection between psychology and religion in the Western world. In the Eastern religions at their highest, the connection was never broken. That the individual can discover for himself that the life we know through our senses is not all: that there is another sphere (Teilhard's noösphere) which transcends it; that what we are now able to see and know is *subjctively* limited by our own "blinded sight,"—a surface manifestation only of the greater reality that lies behind and within the passing flux which we mistake for the whole—this is the most important discovery man can make. It points to the final term in this stage of the evolutionary process. In this discovery lies salvation.

Like the Buddha, and the still earlier Vedantists, Paul taught that we must "work out our own salvation," but he confused the issue by claiming that it was also necessary to believe what he himself believed. The time is ripe for greater flexibility and for a shift of emphasis from believing to becoming.

Living truth, which carries power and authority, must be perceived by the individual himself to be true. We can perceive and understand as we grow only by working at the development of our inner selves. If we fail in this, further evolution of consciousness comes to a standstill, and though outwardly active, we may be inwardly devolving or "dead." For this reason Coomaraswamy said, "I pray that death will not come and catch me unannihilate," meaning, "before I am master of my lower self." For if we are to enter the next dimension, we have to equip ourselves for it, just as the child in the womb has to grow until ready for birth and for breathing in the dimension of air. We have to develop insight as well as intellect, and insight involves what James Hillman calls "insearch," going deeply into the nonconscious part of the mind so that we may discover what it can tell us not only of our instinctive natures but also of our higher potential.

No one has ever suggested that the way of expanding and deepening of consciousness is a clear and easy path. It is more like "groping in an African jungle among the gigantic tangled roots and lianas of good and evil," which is the way McGlashan puts it in *The Savag and Beautiful Country*. He goes on to give us this guidance: "Without relinquishing his social achievements (such as they are), his new psychological insights, and his staggering technical triumphs, man must nevertheless go back to his horn book and learn again the lost alphabet of living. To survive in any meaningful way, he must reawaken the pristine power to see every object and every event translucently — that is, not only as a vividly concrete reality, but also as a semipermeable membrane, through which *another order of experience begins to become manifest,* and to give exactly equal validity to these two aspects of reality's Janus face." This is precisely what the mystic is able to do, to see life Janus-faced; both the face that we know through our senses and the face that is normally hidden from our sight, both the ordinary stuff of everyday living and the "inside" of life.

To know that the world of the senses is but one manifestation of a deeper and more glorious reality, at present beyond the power of our insight to perceive, is to know all that we need to know for our reassurance in this stage of existence. But when the mystics tell us of this other reality we do not quite believe them and decide they are probably deluding themselves with hallucinations and wishful thinking. The loss is ours, because only faith in a larger life can give meaning to this one.

That great lover of reason Socrates, as he grew older, became ever more sure that death was not the end. When waiting for the hemlock, he said in reply to Crito's question as to how he wanted to be buried: "Anyway you like — if you can catch me and I don't get away from you." Then, laughing, he said to the others, "I cannot persuade Crito that I am the same Socrates who has been talking just now.... He thinks I am the dead body he is going to see in a little while."

Likewise the mystic Plotinus wrote in his old age to Flaccus: "I am weary of this prison house the body and calmly await the day when the divine nature within me shall be set free from matter." And when his body was dying he said to his friend Eustocius, "I was waiting for you, before that which is divine in me departs to unite itself with the divine in the universe."

Indian religions have recognized the wisdom of weaning ourselves from worldly possessions and affairs and of dedicating old age to contemplation of "the Beyond that is within." T. S. Eliot gives the same direction:

> Old men ought to be explorers,
> Here or there does not matter
> We must be still and still moving
> Into another intensity
> For a further union.

because if we go on working and exploring, we shall become convinced that as Goethe said, "the spirit is indestructible." He added, "If I work unceasingly to the end, when the present can no longer sustain my spirit, nature is bound to provide me with another form of existence." It is beyond question true that as we become more aware of the spirit dimension, fear of death of the body vanishes proportionately. For, in the words of an earlier mystic poet, Francis Thompson:

> Thus hath He unto death His beauty given:
> And so of all which form inheriteth
> The fall doth pass the rise in worth;
> For birth hath in itself the germ of death,
> But death hath in itself the germ of birth.
> It is the falling acorn buds the tree,
> The falling rain that bears the greenery,
> The fern plants moulder when the ferns arise,
> For there is nothing lives but something dies,
> And there is nothing dies but something lives,
> Till skies be fugitives,
> Till Time, the hidden root of change, updries,
> Are birth and death inseparable on earth;
> For they are twain yet one, and Death is Birth.
>
> "Ode to the Setting Sun"

Epilogue

Fate, that is given to all men partly shaped,
Is ours to alter daily till we die.
JOHN MASEFIELD

This book ends as it began, on a personal note. Looking back on life, I am able to see why the neat little mold that contained my early cosmology had, like the eggshell, to be broken. It was altogether too small and static to allow for growth toward larger horizons; too rigid for me to discover myself as an inherent part of the whole and "God" as the great stream of life that flows through all creation and from which, or "whom," I derive the power to become my own potential self—whatever that may be.

Slowly, through the years, I have come to see that we are all embryonic and transitional creatures in the process of becoming, and that therefore our *raison d'être* in this space-time world is continuous growth and development in the spheres of mind and spirit.

Toward what we grow it is not possible for us to say, any more than it is possible for the grub to envisage the Cloudy Yellow or the Little Chalk Blue that it may become. But the knowledge that there is another dimension or "many dwelling-places" (*John XIV,* 2) to be explored is what gives meaning to life.

As we are at present, we are almost as unaware of a non-material universe within and beyond the world known to us through our senses as were the primitive forms of life unaware of the force fields, electromagnetic and gravitational, that surrounded them. Yet they gradually learned, albeit unconsciously, to respond and adapt to these force fields and to develop the organs—the fins, gills, and light-sensitive cells—necessary to that adaptation. May it not be that as the fish deprived of water struggled to develop lungs through which he could breathe in a strange new medium, so man, struggling in the travail of his soul to find an answer to life's "insoluble" problems, may discover and respond to the force field of spiritual reality, the "noösphere" that surrounds him?

Religious Education

(a) Problems Created for the Child by Conflicting Teaching
Children of today are encouraged to read critically and to think about what they read. It is therefore inevitable that if the Bible is presented to them as a Holy Book of which every word is true, they will ask: "What do I believe—what is in the Bible, or what the Biology teacher tells us?"

In an essay entitled "God and Us." nine-year-old Kevin wrote: "I think it is very difficult for children to decide whether God made the world and Adam and Eve, or if man was made by evolution from monkeys and apes and the world made by gases fusing together.

"People have had different ideas about God.... I am not a very firm believer in Jesus. . . .

"I think I prefer the scientific way because in this way you can find out and tell other people about it, but the other way you can't."

The teaching of the Genesis creation myth as literal truth had caused Kevin to deduce that there are two contradictory approaches to truth, the religious and the scientific, and that the latter is the more reliable. To avoid this conflict, the meaning of the myth should be explained and children should be told of the many other creation myths that have been passed down from early times. *Earth and Sky* and *Beginnings of Life and Death,* both by Sophia Fahs, contain stories of other creation myths.

As they grow older, children should be helped to understand that there are two orders of knowledge and two modes of knowing, the one objective and scientific, the other subjective and intuitive. They do not contradict each other.

The distinction has been finely expressed by Professor G. Lowes Dickenson in *The Magic Flute.* When the young seeker after truth, Tamino, is being examined as to his fitness for entry into the Hall of Sarastro, the Master asks him:

What brings you here?
Tamino: The love of truth.
Sarastro: What do you understand by truth?
Tamino: First truth of fact, and secondly truth of value.
Sarastro: What is the evidence of truth of fact?
Tamino: The perception of the outer senses, enlarged by instruments, corrected by comparison, and related by logic.
Sarastro: What is the evidence of truth of value?
Tamino: The perception of the inner sense, tested and developed by experience.
Sarastro: Is there any other method of truth?
Tamino: There is none.

It is only natural that peoples of different cultures should desire to retain their own differing forms of expression, but children should be taught tolerance of all varied forms, and should also understand that no one of them contains all truth, as the sectarian claims. Teachers should understand that education is religious if it seeks to further growth and development, fosters love of truth and beauty, stirs the imagination, and generates concern for others and the desire to be of use.

A good educational system would do its best to make provision for some degree of contact with the earth, for this is the birthright of every child and as necessary to the soul as food to the body. I have seen an ultramodern comprehensive school generously supplied with tennis courts and free milk but without a tree, a flowerbed, or a quiet path where one might walk alone and find the peace that passes understanding. It was a serious deprivation for which no verbal instruction and no fine glass building could substitute.

(b) Evolution: A Conversation
Walking along the lonely shore one day in late autumn, I came to the small sunny cove where one could shelter from the wind. As I drew near, it was an unpleasant surprise to hear pop music blasting forth, but I disguised my feelings and amiably asked the young couple lying there whether they would mind turning

it down a little. Thereupon the young man jerked his thumb toward the empty beach, remarking curtly, "Plenty of room out there."

"Yes, but it's cold out there."

"Well you've had your life; its our turn now."

Not feeling that I should be written off quite so brusquely at sixty-five, I replied: "But you don't really know what I've had; I may have had a very hard life."

"Well, you've had it anyway."

Something in me refused to give up: "Don't you think you've got your philosophy upside-down?" I asked.

"What d'you mean?"

"I mean your values are misplaced. It matters very much how we live and whether we show consideration for others, regardless of age."

"Why should we? Everything's going to pieces anyway. You've made a mess of the world; why shouldn't we young ones enjoy life and have a good time while we can?"

"That is what the older generation used to say to us when we were your age. They were very shocked and saddened by the First World War and some would admit, "We've made an awful mess of things; it's up to you young people to take over now and find a better way." I expect each generation may go on saying it for some time to come, because to build a new world is not so easy as it sounds. But if humanity fails ultimately, it will be because too many people have opted to live as you say you intend doing—for personal enjoyment only."

"Well, the bomb's going to fall anyway, so what's the use?"

"You may be right; but on the other hand you know the story of the horseshoe; 'for want of a nail the shoe was lost. . . .' You might be that nail. You never can tell what difference a single person might make. And in any case, there's something else."

"What else?"

The tone indicated an awakening of interest. The girl-wife had slowly turned off the transistor radio. I said, "Let us admit that we—mankind in general—have made a mess of things, but there have also been some through the centuries who have done their utmost to make the world a better place, and without their efforts things would be much worse than they are. You wouldn't own that radio set and — more important — you would never have had a chance of getting educated. Doesn't it seem a bit ungrateful to take all and then refuse to carry the torch yourself? Life's a battle, and sometimes the forces of evil win. If you don't play your part, you're a deserter and you will have missed the meaning of it all. We *can* learn how to live together in peace on this planet if enough people will try. To refuse to try, to throw up the sponge because things look so difficult, is to block the evolutionary process and to be unworthy of the great efforts of the past."

> If hopes were dupes, fears may be liars.
> It may be, in yon smoke concealed
> Your comrades chase e'en now the fliers
> And but for you, possess the field.

For the next hour we talked of the evolutionary process and the wonders of the changes that had taken place in the long journey from stardust to man; of the apparent trend in the process toward more mind, and of how further development for conscious man must depend on his conscious choice and effort.

When their hotel gong sounded for lunch we parted on friendly terms. I did not see them again, as their honeymoon was over.

I call this kind of conversation religious education, because it is concerned with what is an essentially religious matter; that is, man's attitude to life and the nature of the choice before him — whether to drift along casually on a materialist basis, uninvolved, with a defeatist outlook, or to struggle upstream toward the source of such values and ideals as we have thus far been able to discover. In its conative aspect religion boils down to this simple choice between going on or drifting back. Religious education, like all true education, will be concerned with helping people to go forward in ways that are positive and creative. It will seek to enlarge men's horizons and stimulate their innate desire to be of use; to arouse in them a sense of responsibility for carrying forward the great life process.

Some Sources of the Enduring Tradition

Jesus was not the first or last to tell men of the Dharma, the true path, the Tao, or the way. The abiding and unshaken tradition is to be found in the teachings of all great religious masters throughout the ages. Some of their words are almost identical.

Jesus said, "What will a man gain by winning the whole world at the cost of his true self?" *(Matthew XVI, 26. N.E.B.)* Gautama, said "Be such as have the self as your lamp, the self as the only refuge" and according to the Vedanta, the oldest of all religions, "Self is Lord of self, and *Tat tvam asi;* thou art that." (Note that the self, true self or high self has the same meaning as the soul.)

Again, Jesus said: "Strait is the gate and narrow is the way that leadeth unto life, and few there be that find it." *(Matthew VII, 14. A.V.)*

Gautama said: "I have seen the ancient way, the old road that was taken by the formerly all-awakened," and, "Difficult is the hearing of the true law; difficult is the birth of the awakened." *(The Dhammapada, 18.)* Lao-tzu says the same in the Tao-te-ching: "Great Tao is very straight, but the people love byways." *(The Tao-te-ching, L, III.)*

To the man piling up wealth for himself, though a pauper in the sight of God, Jesus said: "You fool, this very night you must surrender your life." *(Luke XII, 20.)* "Lay not up for yourselves treasure upon earth." *(Matthew VI, 21.)* The same theme is reflected in the teaching of Jainism: "Again and again it should be repeated...too much attachment to things should be avoided." *(Tattvartha IX, 7.)*

Paul's "Eye hath not seen nor ear heard the things which God hath prepared," *(I Corinthians II, 9.)* corresponds to "The eye of no man has ever seen, nor ever heard, nor do they come into the heart of a man, but God alone reveals them through his spirit." (Komensky, *The Way of Light*, Dedication, 18.) "What a man soweth, that shall he reap," *(Galatians VI, 7.)* was foreshadowed by Tseng-tse: "Beware, Beware! Your actions will recoil on your own head." *(Mencius*, II, 12.) Finally there are the words of the sage Lu Ch'iu: "Restrict your appetites and needs . . . put away all crafty calculations . . . set your heart upon the path . . . Do this, and your heaven (or soul) shall be safe from destruction." *(P'ien*, 14.) Such words of wisdom constitute a part of that tradition known as the "eternal gospel," (Gerald Heard, *The Eternal Gospel*) or the "perennial philosophy," (Aldous Huxley, *The Perennial Philosophy*) the deep core of truth that can be found in all inspired scriptures throughout the ages, including and preceding the Bible. One need not accept all that is written in these scriptures as literally true—only recognize the fact that the same essential thread of eternal truth runs through them all.

The *beliefs and customs* peculiar to any particular thought system are of a different and secondary nature. A man is not saved by his code of beliefs, which are mainly an accident of conditioning, but by finding the inner light of his own true self or soul.

N.B. For all these quotations, other than those from the Bible, I am indebted to the book *Wisdom is One*, a collection of the sayings of some of the Masters, compiled by B. W. Huntsman, published by John M. Watkins.

Index

Abelard, Peter, 77
Abraham, 82
Acts, 123
Adler, Alfred, 48, 122
adolescent growth, 38-46
"AE" (George William Russell), 22
Aeschylus, 138
afterlife, belief in, 58, 153
After the War (Dickenson), 41
agnosticism, 80
Al Hallaj, Sufi, 99
All My Sons (Miller), 42
American Indians, 89, 120
amor santo, 87
anthropomorphism, 83-84, 91
Aristotle, 147, 155
Arnold, Matthew, 24, 85, 128
Aspects of Love (Lilar), 42
Assagioli, Robert, 136
astral bodies, 148
Athanasian Creed, 77, 106
Athanasius, St., 76, 106
atheism, modern, 80, 82
Athenian youth, vow of, 40-41
atonement, doctrine of, 103
Augustine, St., 44,
Aurobindo (Indian mystic), 29, 117, 124
Austen, Mary, 89
authority, belief and, 9

Baal, 84
Bacchae, 43
Bacon, Francis, 154
balance, in Vedanta philosophy, 132
Balfour, Sir Graham, 138
bar mitzvah, 39
Barnes, Bishop Ernest William, 117
becoming, growth and, 62
being, 62
belief: barrier against, 16; religion and, 16-17; *see also* faith

Berdyaev, Nikolai A., 69, 106, 140
Berrill, Norman J., 23, 103
"Beyond," extrasensory perception and, 73; *see also* extrasensory perception; life after death
Bhagavad-Gita, 125, 156
Bianco da Siena, 87
Bible: biology and, 73, 162; children's attitude toward, 137-138; vs. evolution, 16; *see also under individual Books*
birth control, papal encyclical on, 133
Blake, William, 19, 40, 88, 102
blind belief, breakdown of, 9; *see also* belief, faith
body, after death, 58
Boehme, Jacob, 29, 99
Boethius, 29, 47
Boisen, Anton, 34
Bonhoeffer, Dietrich, 101
book, meaning of, 33
Bowlby, John, 49
Brahma, union with, 118
bread of heaven, for spiritual growth, 57
breaking point, self-knowledge at, 39
Broad, Professor, 150
Browning, Robert, 23, 60, 92
Bruno, Giordano, 29, 111
Buber, Martin, 90
Buddha (Gautama Buddha) and Buddhism, 16, 19, 22, 48, 95, 100, 124-126, 139, 143, 157, 166; vs. Christianity, 120-121
Bucke, Richard M., 71
Burt, Cyril, 147

capacity, latent or potential, 33
carnal desires, 42
Cary, Joyce, 137
Catholic Church, 76, 142
Cavell, Edith, 111

Chekhov, Anton, 9
childhood: forced growth in, 38; hindrances to growth in, 35-37; transition to manhood from, 38-39; "unwanted" feeling in, 36
Chinese artists, 89
Christadelphians, 101
Christianity: atonement doctrine in, 103; vs. Buddhism, 120-121; essence of, 101; Jesus in, 95; mythological symbolism in, 21; "salvation" in, 143; in West, 68-69
Christmas, meaning of, 21
Church, Richard, 72
Clarke, Sir James, 48
Clarke, Ronald W., 86
Coast, John, 121
Cobb, Geikie, 101
Collin, Rodney, 147-148
communication, feeling and, 126
conscious action, vs. unconscious motivation, 49
Conze, Edward, 120
Cook, George C., 57
Coomaraswamy, Ananda, 158
Corinthians, 155, 166
cortex, overdevelopment of, 107
Cosmic Consciousness, 71-72
cosmic duty, 27
cosmic provincialism, 27
cosmology, religion and, 73
cosmos, as interrelated organism, 28
Council of Nicaea, 97
courage, ideal of, 40
Cousins, Norman, 131, 143
Cox, Edwin, 24
Creative Force, 76
creative living, art of, 156-160

Dante Aligheri, 74, 138
Darwin, Charles, 30

Davis, Charles, 141
death: fear of, 145, 154-156; as gate of life, 148, 156; as great transition, 145-152; inner significance of, 153-160; as life process, 149; meaning of, 24; spiritual self after, 58
deep self, growth from, 54-59
Depth Psychology and Modern Man (Progoff), 34, 110
"descent into hell," 34
"Devourer," Florence Nightingale and, 48
Dewey, John, 113
Dickens, Charles, 50
Dickenson, G. Lowes, 41, 162-163
Dionysus, 43
discipline, 44
divine flame, 57, 75, 110
Divine Flame, The (Hardy), 73
Dixon, Macneile, 150
doctrinal differences, religious unity and, 117-128
Doll's House, The (Ibsen), 50
doubt, and transition to faith, 15-22
dreams, 54-55
"drifter" type, 34
drinking, escape in, 34
dropouts from life, 34
drugs: ecstasy through, 71; escape in, 34

Easter, meaning of, 21
Eastern religions, 22, 125-126
Ecclesiastes, 23, 154
Eckhart, Meister, 29, 85, 106
ecstasy, drugs and, 71
Edison, Thomas A., 150
education: "omnipotence" of, 24; for youth, 45
Eightfold Path, 125
Einstein, Albert, 25, 70, 91

Eiseley, Loren, 74, 94, 138
Eliade, Mircea, 156
Eliot, T. S., 52, 69, 159
Emerson, Ralph Waldo, 47
emotional illness, growth blockage in, 36
empathic understanding, 126
endurance contests, 39-40
energy, uncontrolled, 40
Ephesians, 20, 103
erotic love, 43
ESP, see extrasensory perception
"Essay on Man" (Pope), 52
eternal life, 147-148
Euripides, 29
evil, God and, 43, 92
evolution, 161; Bible and, 16; human isolation and, 27; and man's function in universe, 27; mind as culmination of, 25; religion and, 73, 163-165; "desacrilized, 156
existence: meaning of, 29; purpose of, 24
existential vacuum, 16
experience, God and, 17
extrasensory perception (ESP), 73, 147, 152
Ezekiel, 18

Fahs, Sophia, 162
"failure of nerve," 61
faith: breakdown of, 24; loss of, 15-22, 134-135; religious life and, 62; transition from doubt to, 15-22
"false face," 50
family, importance of, 42
Fausset, Hugh L'Anson, 67
feeling, 126
fire: life of, 56; as Promethean gift, 57
Forsyte Saga, The (Galsworthy), 68
Fosdick, Harry Emerson, 117
Frankl, Viktor, 136, 157
Freud, Anna, 49
Freud, Sigmund, 48, 54, 81, 136, 143, 147
Frost, Robert, 58
frustrated development, 36
Fuller, Richard Buckminster, 28
Future of an Illusion, The (Freud), 136

Gabriel, "glory" of, 61
Gabriel and the Creatures (Heard), 60

Galatians, 122, 167
Galileo, 147
Gandhi, Mohandas K., 119
Garrison, William Lloyd, 111
Gautama Buddha, see Buddha and Buddhism
Ghost in the Machine (Koestler), 49
Gill, Winifred, 81
God: absence of, 81; anthropomorphic, 81-83, 125; as center of centers, 51; changing concepts of, 79-81; of childhood, 22, 82-83; conscious intelligence of, 85; as creative principle, 88; as Creator and Destroyer, 92; "death" of, 80; deduction of, 85-86; development of ideas about, 83-84; doubts about, 79; evil and, 43, 92; as "exalted Father," 81; existence of, 19; experience and, 17-18; faith in, 153; as Father, 77-93, 133; as Great Watchmaker, 79; as guide, 59; as harmony, 91; as Holy Ghost, 106-116; honesty with, 47; ignorance of, 84-85; immanence of, 75, 87-89, 109-110; inductive approach to, 85-87; as Inner Light, 75; Jesus Christ as, 48, 135; kingdom of, 84, 102; longing for knowledge of, 15; loss of belief in, 106; love from, 86; as moral imperative, 91; mystic view of, 88, 98; Nature and, 80; new concept of, 46; noninvolvement of, 80; old images of, 87; in Old Testament, 137; personal, 19; as power, 83; as Reality, 70, 85; relationship with man, 90-93; search for, 16-17; as Spirit, 90; as supreme person, 106; union with, 88, 98, 118; as Unknown, 70; as Word or Logos, 72, 121
Goddard, Harold, 149
gods of Greece and Rome, 96
Goethe, Johann Wolfgang von, 29, 32, 58, 159
good and evil, problem of, 49, 92-93, 106-108
"grades of significance," 32
Graham, Billy, 83, 101
Great Mother, 133
great transition, 145-160; see also death
Greek gods, 96

Griffiths, Father Bede, 114
growth: adolescent, 38-46; becoming
  and, 62; emotional illness and, 36;
  failure in, 33, 36; goal of, 60-63;
  hindrances to in childhood, 35-37;
  inner, 32-34, 131; as natural to man,
  34; through self-knowledge, 47-
  53; suicide and, 37; vs. tradition,
  131
gunas, 132

Hahn, Kurt, 39-40
half-believers, 24
Hall, D. J., 89
Hallaj, *see* Al Hallaj
Hardy, Sir Alister, 73, 115
harmony, God as, 91
Havens, Teresina, 125
Heard, Gerald, 60, 167
Heaven, glimpse of, 17-18
Hebrews, 70, 122
hell: descent into, 34; as fire and
  brimstone, 57
Helvetius, Claude Adrien, 24
Hemming, James, 49
Henley, William Ernest, 45
henotheism, 84
Heraclitus, 32
Herbart, Johann Friedrich, 142
Herrick, Robert, 35
Hesychius of Jerusalem, 44-45
Hillman, James, 143, 158
Hindu philosophy and religion, 19,
  119
Holy Ghost, God as, 106-116; *see also*
  Holy Spirit
Holy Office, as "scandal," 142
Holy Spirit: as fire, 56-57; Trinity and,
  20
Holy Spirit of Life, 9
Homer, 138
hominization, 108
Hort, Greta, 114
"Hound of Heaven, The" (Thomp-
  son), 114
Hügel, Baron Friedrich von, 69, 101
humanism, 24
human nature, study of, 45
Human Situation, The (Dixon), 158
humility, 127
Huntsman, B. W., 167

Huxley, Aldous, 33, 54, 62-63, 113,
  123, 167
Huxley, Julian, 25, 27, 74, 86, 102,
  113, 145
Huxley, Thomas Henry, 86
hypnotism, 73

Ibsen, Henrik, 51, 109
idealists, philosophic, 30
ideas, history of, 83
Iliad (Homer), 29
Illumination, 71
Immense Journey, The (Eiseley), 74, 138
immortality, 147-148
imperialism, 123
Incarnation, 98, 102
Indians, American, 89
Inge, Dean William Ralph, 117
inner growth, 32-34
inner life, 126
insecurity, self-ignorance and, 49-50
insight, 59
invisible world, 29
Iroquois Indians, 89
Isaac, 82
Isaiah, 43
I-Thou relationship, 90

Jalalu'd-din Rumi, 153
James, William, 115, 147
Janus, 158
Japan, "divine" Emperor of, 132
Jeans, James H., 58
Jehovah, 43, 82
Jehovah's Witnesses, 101
Jesus Christ, 18, 21, 48, 116, 166; as
  beneficial mutation, 94; Christianity
  and, 102, 121; doctrines surrounding, 102; as God, 48, 135; as "godlike human," 98; "gospel" of, 100;
  as "higher consciousness," 95; immortality of, 148; "life within" of,
  103-104; as "man fully himself,"
  97, as Messiah, 94; metaphysical
  nature of, 104; "miracles" of, 99;
  parables of, 103; as prototype, 94-
  105; and religions of East and West,
  95-96; resurrection of, 155; as
  "son of God," 95; in theology, 96;
  true religion and, 70; as "The
  Truth," 99

Jews, as chosen people, 82
Job, 154
John, 95, 99, 101, 104, 116, 154, 161
Johnson, James Weldon, 91
Johnson, Samuel, 30
John the Baptist, 56
Jonah, 91-92
Jowett, Benjamin, 138
Jung, Carl, 21, 23, 48, 55, 93, 100, 106, 110, 120, 126, 143

Kabir (Hindu poet), 29, 143
Kafka, Franz, 33
Kant, Immanuel, 75
Keats, John, 76
Kennedy, John F., 127
Keynes, Maynard, 140
King, Martin Luther, 62
Kingdom of God, 84
"Kingdom of God, The" Thompson), 70
"Kingdom of God within," 102
Kings, 84
Kirtley, 113, 115
Knight, Margaret, 67
knowledge, scientific method and, 142
Koestler, Arthur, 49
Komensky, Jan Amos, 167
Koran, 153
Krishnamurti, Jiddu, 68

Lao-tzu, 89, 109, 125
Laplace, Pierre Simon de, 79
Laski, M., 71
latent capacity, 33
Lawrence, D. H., 36
life: death and, 149; depths of, 44; different interpretations of, 118-119; growth and, 131; as interrelated organisms, 28; meaning of, 23, 30
life after death, 58, 153
Life Divine, The (Aurobindo), 29
Life Force: 27; direction of, 32
Lilar, Suzanne, 42-43
Lipschitz, Jacob, 127
living, art of, 156-157
logotherapy, 28, 136
love: absence of, 86; as "cement," 90; civilizing value of, 43; emotional health and, 50; for God, 86; misconceptions about, 36

Loyola, St. Ignatius of, 16
Lu Ch'iu, 167
Luke, 60

McAllister, David, 118
McCord, James, 135
MacTaggart, John M., 80
Magic Flute, The (Dickenson), 162-163
man: as "belonging to universe," 28; as "child of Cain," 143; challenge to, 26-27; complexity of, 35; "cosmic duty" of, 27, 75; dual allegiance of, 115; at "end of tether," 26; God's immanence in, 87-89; growth necessary in, 32-34; inequality of, 94-105; as part of universe, 58; as person, 35; relationship to God, 90-93; universal, 122
manhood, transition to, 38-39
Margenau, Henry, 146
Mark, 51, 124
Martin, Kingsley, 140-141
Masefield, John, 161
May, Rollo, 33
Matthew, 99, 166
meaning: roads to, 23-31; through religion, 67-128; through transition, 129-160
Méchanique Céleste, La (Laplace), 79
Micklem, N., 99
milieu divin, 26
Miller, Arthur, 42
mind: as blank sheet, 51-52; as culmination of evolution, 25; sphere of, 26
Modern Man in Search of a Soul (Jung), 110
moment of truth, 29
Montaigne, Michel Eyquem de, 48
Moses, 124
mother, possessive, 36
murder, "love" and, 43
Murray, Gilbert, 147
mystic consciousness, paraconsciousness and, 72
Mysticism (Underhill), 71, 88
Mysticism and Logic (Russell), 112
mysticism and mystic experience, 21, 70; "spirit field" and, 113-114; union with God in, 88, 98, 118; wonder and, 74

Myth and Ritual in Christianity (Watts), 98

natural, vs. supernatural, 30
natural theology, 25
nature, God's immanence in, 87-89
Navajo religion, 118
Nehru, B. K., 124
Nehru, Jawaharlal, 141
nerve, failure of, 61
Neumann, Erich, 133
neurosis, growth failure and, 33
New Statesman, The (Hemming), 49
Newton, Sir Isaac, 79, 84
Nietzsche, Friedrich, 23, 30, 37, 48, 138
Nightingale, Florence, 48
Nirvana, 71, 115
noösphere, 26, 29, 57, 157, 161
Norah, Ibsen character, 50
noumenal, experience of, 17

Odin, 44
Old Testament, 55; *see also* Bible
Orgel, Irene, 91
orgies, Dionysus and, 43
Origins and History of Consciousness (Neumann), 133
Otto, Rudolf, 22
Ouspensky, P. D., 15
Over the Bridge (Church), 72

Parable of the Sower, 103
paraconsciousness, 72
parapsychology, 21, 147
Paris Academy of Sciences, 150
Pascal, Blaise, 17
Pater, Walter, 76
patriotism, 42
Paul, St., 19-20, 52, 70, 122, 148, 155-158, 166
peace, desire for, 41
Pentecost, 56
Pharisees, 50
Phenomène Humaine, Le (Teilhard de Chardin), 25, 108
Philip of Spain, 122
Philippians, 52
philosophic idealists, 30
Plato, 155
Plotinus, 29, 63, 116, 159
Pope, Alexander, 52

possessive mother, 36-37
potential capacity, 33
Potter, Beatrix, 33
pragmatic test, 115
precognition, 73
Price, H. H., 152
Princeton Theological Seminary, 135
Progoff, Ira, 34, 54, 103, 109
Prospero, in *Tempest*, 54
Psalms, 18, 94, 153
psyche: division in, 49; dreams and, 54-55; infant, 50; suffering and, 157
psychosis, growth failure and, 33
psychosynthesis, 136
psychotherapy, new forms of, 136

Quakers, 125
Quest of the Historical Jesus, The (Schweitzer), 139

Radhakrishnan, Sir Sarvepali, 32, 67, 127-128
rajas, 132
Ramsey, Arthur Michael, Archbishop of Canterbury, 87
rationalism, 29
reality, "frequency" and, 151
real person, 100-101
religion: "advanced beliefs" in, 119; ambiguity of word, 67; belief and, 16-17, 68; as "beyond reach," 70; Christianity and, 69; contemporary interpretations of, 67-75; "efficiency" of, 128; evolution and, 73, 163-165; faith and, 62-63; as growth, 138; humanism and, 112-113; Jesus and, 70; life spirit and, 127; meaning through, 67-128; as mystic experience, 70; philosophic, 69; quality and, 68; revelation and, 74-75; science and, 73, 112-113; theological doctrines and, 67
religious education, 162-165
religious philosophy, need for, 45
religious unity: doctrines and, 117-128; psychological hindrances to, 122-128
revelation, religion and, 74-75
Rexroth, Kenneth, 29
Rilke, Rainer Maria, 81
Rishis (Hindu sages), 68

Robinson, Bishop John A., 47, 81, 97
Robinson, Ruth, 138
Roman gods, 96
Romans, 95, 155
Rubenstein, Rabbi R. L., 80
Ruskin, John, 52
Russell, Bertrand, 112, 145
Russell, George William ("AE"), 22

Samuel, 84
Satori, 71, 115
sattva, 132
Saul, 122; *see also* Paul, St.
Savage and Beautiful Country, The (McGlashan), 158
Schonfield, Hugh, 131
Schweitzer, Albert, 96, 104, 139
science, religion and, 9, 73, 112, 145-152
Search, The (Snow), 71
Second Commandment, 84
self, growth of, 53-59
self-conquest, need for, 45
self-dedication, 40
self-discipline, 116
selfhood, function of, 51
self-ignorance, danger of, 47
self-knowledge, 104; growth through, 47-53; tests of, 39
self-observation, 116
self-sacrifice, God as, 86
self-transformation, 104
self-worth, 45
Sense and Thought (Hort), 114
service, 42
sex impulses, 42
sexual education, 44
Shakespeare, William, 21, 33, 54
Shankara (Shankaracharya), 29, 117
Shaw, George Bernard, 32
Shiva, 43, 92
Sidwick, Henry, 147
significance, grades of, 32
Silesius, Angelus, 89
sin, 119
Smith, John, 79
Smith, Rev. Gregor, 80
"smother love," 36
Smuts, Jan Christian, 103
Snow, C. P., 71
Socrates, 21, 48, 100, 139, 159
Sophocles, 138

Spinoza, 29, 91
spire, 56
spirit: as culmination of evolution, 25; dimensions of, 106-116; immanence of, 140; relationship of, 111; sphere or world of, 26, 30
"spiritual body," 148
spiritual experience, 142
spiritual "field," 31, 113
spiritualism, death and, 145
spiritual self, 53
Spurgeon, C. H., 15, 71
square "carriage," 55-56
stardust, man and, 74
Stark, Freya, 131
Streeter, Burnett H., 85
suffering, "reason" for, 23
Sufi teachers, 38
suicide, growth failure and, 37
Suicide and Soul (Hillman), 143
sun worship, 83
supernatural, as extension of natural, 30
Supreme Being, existence of, 19; *see also* God

Tagore, Sir Rabindranath, 29, 119
tamas, 132-133
technocracy, "omnipotence" of, 25
Teilhard de Chardin, Pierre, 25, 51, 107, 142, 157
telepathy, 73, 152
Temple, Archbishop Frederick, 136
Temple, Archbishop William, 81
Tennyson, Alfred Lord, 44, 114
Thant, U, 122
theological doctrines, religion and, 67
theology, natural, 25
Theory of Eternal Life, The (Collin), 147
Thompson, Francis, 70, 112, 114, 160
Thou relationship, 90
thought, integrative, 59
"Tiger, The" (Blake), 19
Tillich, Paul, 68
totalitarianism, 119-120, 123, 127
tradition: sources of, 166-167; transition and, 131-144
tragedy, God's permission of, 20
transition: meaning through, 131-160; tradition and, 131-144
tree, symmetry of, 58

tree of life, 57
"Tree of My Window" (Frost), 58
Trinity, 20, 77
true self, difficulty in becoming, 100
truth, as religion, 119
Tseng-tse, 167
Turner, Joseph M. W., 33

Unamuno, Jugo Miguel de, 100
uncertainty principle, 146-147
unconscious motivation, vs. conscious
    action, 49
Underhill, Evelyn, 71, 88, 118, 143
Undiscovered Self, The (Jung), 21
unhappiness, bearing with, 23
universe: nonmaterial, 161; "unob-
    structed," 151-152
Unobstructed Universe, The (White), 151
Upanishads, 118
Uriah Heep character, 50
uroboric incest, 133

Vaughan, Henry, 72
Vedanta philosophy, 118, 125, 132,
    140, 157
Ved Mehta, 81
Virgin Birth, 102
Virgin Mary, 76
Vivekananda, 124
"Voices of the Lord," 28
volcano, 56
Voltaire, 111

Waiting for Godot (Beckett), 134
Waley, Arthur, 88
Walker, Kenneth, 99, 118
Wallace, Alfred Russel, 30

war: history and, 107; futility of, 41;
    self-ignorance and, 49
Ward, Barbara, 95-96
Watkins, John M., 167
Watts, Alan, 98, 101, 117-118
Wells, H. G., 26, 57
Western mind, religion and, 126
Weyl, Herman, 111
Wheelwright, Mary Cabot, 118
White, Stewart Edward, 151
Whitehead, Alfred North, 29, 62, 69-
    70, 88, 112, 149-150
Whitehorn, Katherine, 91
Wilderness of the Lost, drifter and, 34
Williams, H. A., 97
Wilson, Canon J. M., 79
wisdom, 134
womb, return to, 133
wonder, sense of, 74
Wordsworth, William, 24, 38
work, need for, 69
world, remolding of, 45
world community, world religion and,
    9
World Council of Churches, 140
"world invisible," 29
world of spirit, 30, 106-116
World War I, disillusionment of, 40-
    41
worship, psychological need for, 96

yoga, 45, 116
You and the Universe (Berrill), 103
young people or youth: education of,
    45; purpose and existence for, 24;
    "splendid urge" of, 38-39

Zabolgi, 85
Zen Buddhism, 62, 143